Thirsty

Thirsty

12 WEEKS
of DRINKING DEEPLY
from GOD'S WORD

HANNAH C. HALL

Revell

a division of Baker Publishing Group
Grand Rapids, Michigan

Published by Revell
a division of Baker Publishing Group
PO Box 6287, Grand Rapids, MI 49516-6287
www.revellbooks.com

Printed in the United States of America

Library of Congress Cataloging-in-Publication Data
Names: Hall, Hannah C., author.
Title: Thirsty : 12 weeks of drinking deeply from God's word / Hannah C. Hall.
Description: Grand Rapids : Revell, a division of Baker Publishing Group, [2022] | Includes
    bibliographical references.
Identifiers: LCCN 2021045553 | ISBN 9780800740191 (cloth) | ISBN 9781493434367 (ebook)
Subjects: LCSH: Bible—Meditations.
Classification: LCC BS491.5 .H345 2022 | DDC 242/.5—dc23
LC record available at https://lccn.loc.gov/2021045553

The author is represented by the Apokedak Literary Agency.

Baker Publishing Group publications use paper produced from sustainable forestry practices and post-consumer waste whenever possible.

Interior design by William Overbeeke.

22   23   24   25   26   27   28   7   6   5   4   3   2   1

For my pray-ers:
Jennifer, Sally, and Mom.

And for Josh, my love.

"I thank my God every time I remember you"
(Phil. 1:3 NIV).

Proverbs

Romans 8

... the God of God ...

Romans 15:13

Psalm 1:1–3

2 Chronicles 20:12

1 Peter 3:3–4

Nehemiah 8:10

2 Corinthians 5:21

John 15:5

Proverbs 19:21

Romans 8:1–2

1 Thessalonians 5:16–18

Nahum 1:7

Colossians 3:1–3

Proverb...

Rom...

CONTENTS

INTRODUCTION

I'll never forget the moment it happened.

It was a normal day. I stood at the kitchen sink doing the same thing I did every day, three times a day, forever and ever, amen. I washed dishes.

A young wife and mom, I had a good, easy-ish life. I did what women with good, easy-ish lives do. I cared for my family's needs. I loved my husband and submitted (sometimes) to his leadership. I read my Bible. I served in church. I had no reason to question my existence, nor did it seem like prime time for a major spiritual crisis.

But then it happened.

Like a rude and uninvited guest, a question barged into my mind. Coming out of nowhere, it suddenly crowded out every other thought, elbowed its way to the front, and bellowed its frustration.

This is the abundant life? Really?

How disappointing.

I stopped scrubbing, shocked at myself. Where had that come from? Was it true? Did I really feel that way?

I knew enough to know that my question was based on something Jesus had said. "The thief comes only to steal and kill and destroy. I came that they may have life and have it abundantly" (John 10:10).

Good news, right? Jesus promised his followers abundance. *Life to the full.* Which, in Jesus-speak, can be translated to mean overflowing joy, peace that passes understanding, guidance from the Holy Spirit, powerful and effective prayers, faith strong enough to move mountains, hope that abounds despite our circumstances . . .

All of which was foreign to me.

Life was good, but it wasn't abundant. I was missing out. And I do not like missing out.

The problem, I knew, was not on Jesus's end. The Bible is true, its words without error. Any disappointment I was experiencing was not a failure on God's part but on mine.

For years I had skimmed, snoozed through, and skipped around in Scripture. I'd even started and stopped an embarrassingly impressive number of Bible reading plans. But these herky-jerky approaches to my quiet time had done me no favors.

I remembered another promise Jesus had made—to a woman he met at a well—that, should she just ask, he would give her a gift: *living water.* She never had to be thirsty again (John 4:10–14).

Suddenly I knew—with such clarity I couldn't believe I hadn't realized it sooner—that I wanted more. I wanted abundance. *Fullness.* I longed to be satisfied in Christ. I needed living water.

I was thirsty.

And it was time to do something about it.

But how?

Let's just be honest: I wasn't in a season of life when I could reasonably rearrange my days to work in hours of personal Bible study. The devotionals I tried seemed fluffy and light on doctrine, but heavy-duty Bible studies overwhelmed me.

I needed a way to dig into Scripture that was doable for a busy woman but deep enough for a thirsty soul.

And God was gracious.

Hannah, reading the Bible is not a race to the finish. (The voice of God sounds an awful lot like the voice of reason sometimes, doesn't it?)

It's okay to take it slow.

And my whole spirit sighed *deeply.*

What God revealed to me in the days and weeks after that moment was not a fresh, bold concept but rather an ancient spiritual discipline, often overlooked but oh so practical.

Scripture meditation.

Beloved, we are allowed—nay, *encouraged*—to slow down and savor truth, one passage, one verse, one word at a time.

Flashy? No.

Effective? *Oh my goodness, yes.*

Through my meditation on Scripture, God worked to rearrange my heart. I learned to drink deeply and intentionally from the pages of the Bible, and he opened my eyes to riches that I would have never seen had I not slowed down to look. Linger. Enjoy.

Scripture meditation is not fast and furious, but it *is* sweet and fruitful.

Not so sure? *Just give me twelve weeks.*

We'll read the same verse or brief passage together each week. Every day of that week, in a short devotional, we will pause to look at, linger over, and enjoy what God says. We'll study to understand, prayerfully ask God to reveal, and boldly believe that we will be changed by the truths we discover.

Best of all, we will slowly begin to lose our good, easy lives as we joyfully find better, abundant lives in Christ.

There will still be dishes to do. Life will probably always be busy. And there will be a million reasons not to sit ourselves down and soak in the Word.

But now we'll know better.

Because once we've tasted and seen God's goodness and the all-satisfying abundance he offers us in Christ, we'll know we'd have to be crazy not to drink as deeply and as often from that sweet living water as we possibly can.

One of my favorite verses, Psalm 90:14, is my daily prayer: "Satisfy us in the morning with your unfailing love, that we may sing for joy and be glad all our days" (NIV). Another version translates that first line, "Let thy love dawn on us undimmed" (Moffatt).

Yes! This is my prayer for us too.

Lord, we are thirsty. Satisfy us with yourself. Dawn on us fresh every morning with your undimmed love. Pour out on us, Father, so that we, your beloved daughters, may sing for joy and be glad in you all our days. Amen.

And together, I believe we will say, "We've drank deeply and we're satisfied. Life in Christ truly is fully, wonderfully, beautifully abundant."

Week 1

PSALM 1:1–3

In all that he does, he prospers. Blessed is the man who walks not in the counsel of the wicked, nor stands in the way of sinners, nor sits in the seat of scoffers; but his delight is in the law of the LORD, and on his law he meditates day and night. He is like a tree planted by streams of water that yields its fruit in its season, and its leaf does not wither.

DAY 1

Blessed is the man who walks not in the counsel of the wicked, nor stands in the way of sinners, nor sits in the seat of scoffers; but his delight is in the law of the LORD, and on his law he meditates day and night. He is like a tree planted by streams of water that yields its fruit in its season, and its leaf does not wither. In all that he does, he prospers.

PSALM 1:1–3

Not too many years ago, I was a dedicated disciple of what author Jen Wilkin refers to as the "Pinball Approach" to Bible reading.[1] Unsure of what to read each day and not disciplined enough to plan it out beforehand, I'd randomly open the Word and pick whatever Scripture my eyes landed on. The next day I'd do the same.

I'd pinball from passage to passage without any thought to where I was headed or where I had been. It was a brilliant way to ensure that my daily Bible reading had little to no impact on my daily life.

I was the person James described as a hearer of the Word but not a doer (James 1:22). You know, the gal who looks at herself in the mirror but then walks away and immediately forgets about the spinach nestled in her teeth. Why bother looking if I'm not going to be changed by what I see?

Trouble was, my problem went deeper than just being forgetful.

I was moving too fast through Scripture and not meditating on what I was reading. I wasn't wrestling with the truths I was discovering or checking my heart to see if I believed them. I certainly wasn't allowing the Holy Spirit time to reveal my sin and change me.

I was checking "Daily Bible Reading" off my list and assuming that was enough.

It wasn't. And before long, the lack of spiritual nourishment in my life began to show.

I love that one Hebrew word for "meditation" (*hagah*) is the same as a Hebrew word translated "growl" in Isaiah 31:4—like a lion roaring over its prey, establishing its possession of it, undaunted by any distractions.[2] *I wanted this. I fought for this. This is mine.*

Though it may sound boring or uncomfortable at first, meditating on Scripture is a fearsome thing in a believer's life. It's being so hungry for truth that we fight for it. Take possession of it. Believe it. We make it ours. And we're changed.

It's an intentional pursuit with Christ as its prize.

It won't be easy.

But let's try it anyway, shall we?

Let's slow down and savor this together. God's Word is absolutely worth the fight.

1 · Write Psalm 1:1–3 on a note card and work on memorizing it this week. Hiding the Word in your heart will prove to be a beneficial and long-lasting companion to your time of meditation.

2 · Think about the connection between the Hebrew word for "meditation" and a lion's growl. How does this change your perspective on Scripture meditation?

DAY 2

Blessed is the man who walks not in the counsel of the wicked, nor stands in the way of sinners, nor sits in the seat of scoffers; but his delight is in the law of the LORD, and on his law he meditates day and night. He is like a tree planted by streams of water that yields its fruit in its season, and its leaf does not wither. In all that he does, he prospers.   PSALM 1:1–3

I recently sprained my ankle. I was jogging, it was dark, and I was on a dirt road. (Upon reflection, it's not the most brilliant combo ever.)

I used to think that skunks and stray dogs were my greatest threats on my morning runs, but my main problem has turned out to be far less exciting.

Potholes. Those suckers will sneak up on you.

That day, I let my eyes stray off the path directly in front of me—the small area illuminated by my headlamp—and I paid for it.

Our psalmist, David, also knew the hazards of taking his eyes off the road. "Your word," he sang, "is a lamp to my feet and a light to my path" (Ps. 119:105).

I know now what David knew then. It's dangerous out there in the world without some illumination.

David had only the first five books of the Bible to read—which are called "the Law" or "Torah." *Torah* means "direction" or "instruction."

David valued these directions from the Lord so much that he tells us in our verses this week that the man who delights in them and meditates on them is blessed.

"Blessed" here isn't some generic hashtag or cultural catchphrase. It's not referring to material or financial success either. Rather, "blessed" is an exclamation of joy that means "Oh, how happy!" or "Oh, the best!"[1]

As in, *Oh, how happy* are we when we delight in God's instruction. *Oh, the best* it is for those who meditate on God's Word.

To David, the Law wasn't some dreary list of rules to follow or study begrudgingly. He *delighted* in it.

I confessed to a friend once that I didn't know how to make myself suddenly start loving my daily Bible reading, and she reminded and reassured me that I could ask God for anything—including that he would help me delight in his Word.

It's a prayer worth praying and one I'm fairly certain God loves answering.

He certainly did for me.

Oh, how happy it is that we have the whole of Scripture to give us instruction, light the dark paths ahead of us, refresh us with God's love, and point us, again and again, to Jesus.

We are blessed, indeed.

1. Do you delight in reading God's Word, or does it feel like a chore to you? Ask God to give you a desire for his Word. Trust him that he will.

2. Think about what we consider "blessed" to mean and what God calls "blessed." Be honest—are you disappointed? Ask him to help you delight and find joy in his deeper, better version of "blessed."

DAY 3

Blessed is the man who walks not in the counsel of the wicked, nor stands in the way of sinners, nor sits in the seat of scoffers; but his delight is in the law of the LORD, and on his law he meditates day and night. He is like a tree planted by streams of water that yields its fruit in its season, and its leaf does not wither. In all that he does, he prospers.   PSALM 1:1–3

An empty-nester friend of mine was recently reflecting on the long days at home with a growing family. "You just gotta keep slinging chow," she said with a laugh.

I laughed too . . . but not quite as hard as she did. It hit a little too close to home, you know?

As soon as I clean the kitchen, it's time to cook again. My people are always eating. Three times a day. It's ridiculous.

Though I'm certain that serving my family is my primary calling right now, there are moments in this season when I wonder what—other than temporarily full bellies—I am producing here. Is there going to be any fruit from all this work? Why can't I see it yet? When, if ever, will all this labor pay off?

David, I think, must have understood my frustration.

He lived in a dry, arid land. Because rainfall wasn't a guarantee, fruit trees needed to be purposefully planted near a water source. These healthy trees could then grow to produce delicious food for people to enjoy.

But it certainly didn't happen immediately.

Newly planted fruit trees can take *years* to bear their first crop. Before those blossoms form, trees will appear to be barren and unproductive. Fruitless.

This time of barrenness is necessary in the life cycle of the tree. It's not an indication that the tree isn't healthy, just that bearing fruit requires maturity. And maturity takes time. *Good fruit* takes time.

I can be so impatient. I hustle and strive to be productive at home or in ministry and then expect to see the fruits of my labor immediately. Yet we all know how disappointing it is to bite into a firm peach or a green banana. You just can't rush good fruit. It's always best enjoyed *in season*. Not too early. Not before it's ready.

While we wait to see the fruit in our marriages, our jobs, our children, or our ministries, purposeful planting in the Word is necessary. Jesus said, "As the branch cannot bear fruit by itself, unless it abides in the vine, neither can you, unless you abide in me" (John 15:4).

After we've been faithful to feed ourselves off of God's Word in the waiting, fruit will come at just the right time. And it will be beautiful. Lovely. Satisfying.

Faithfulness yields fruitfulness. So hold fast, beloved. Good fruit cannot be rushed.

1. Are you in a time of waiting? What can you learn about God in times of waiting that you don't necessarily learn in times of fruitfulness?

_____

_____

_____

2. The funny (or frustrating?) thing about fruit is that it's not grown for the tree to enjoy. It's always meant for someone else. Read Galatians 5:22–23 about the fruit of the Spirit. If this fruit is not for us, who must God have in mind to benefit from our seasons of fruitfulness?

_____

_____

DAY 4

Blessed is the man who walks not in the counsel of the wicked, nor stands in the way of sinners, nor sits in the seat of scoffers; but his delight is in the law of the LORD, and on his law he meditates day and night. He is like a tree planted by streams of water that yields its fruit in its season, and its leaf does not wither. In all that he does, he prospers.   PSALM 1:1–3

In a basic economics class at my Christian college, we held a debate: "Is it okay for Christians to be rich?"

I was assigned to argue on the side of the affirmative. My team contended that God confirmed our position because he had blessed men like Abraham, Job, and Solomon with great material prosperity.

The other side's rebuttal came quickly: "And what about Jesus?"

They had a point.

Our passage this week tells us that the one who meditates on and delights in Scripture will prosper in all he does. This wasn't just wishful thinking or an unsubstantiated promise. God himself had assured Joshua, Moses's successor as leader of the Israelites, that if he would meditate on the law and obey it carefully, he would also be "prosperous and successful" (Josh. 1:8).

But shouldn't Jesus have been prosperous if anyone was? And what of the many biblical and modern examples of people who, despite loving the Lord, not only have not been "successful" but also have experienced incredible suffering or poverty?

Where was their promised prosperity?

The answer is simple. God holds to an entirely different definition of prosperity than our world does. As is often the case with our heavenly Father, his idea of prospering and success may seem a bit upside down.

C. H. Spurgeon elaborates: "Our worst things are often our best things. . . . There is blessing concealed in the righteous man's crosses, losses, and sorrows. The trials of the saint are a divine husbandry, by which he grows and brings forth abundant fruit."[1]

There it is again. Fruit.

Prosperity—in God's economy—may or may not mean we ever achieve material, financial, or ministry success, and there's a strong chance either way we will still face suffering, losses, and sorrows.

But, without a doubt, God's prosperity promise includes a 100 percent guarantee that when we delight in and meditate on Scripture, God will produce in us eternal, life-giving, soul-satisfying fruit.

God determines and defines prosperity, and when we align our lives with him, we can know that we will benefit from this promise.

No, prosperity will likely not be what we expected.

It will be better.

1. Can you think of a time when one of your worst things actually became one of your best things? What did God teach you through that experience?

_____

_____

2. Psalm 32:1 says, "Blessed is the one whose transgression is forgiven, whose sin is covered." Try substituting "Oh, the best" or "Oh, how happy" into the place of "blessed" in the verse. How does this help confirm God's definition of *prosperity*?

_____

_____

DAY 5

Blessed is the man who walks not in the counsel of the wicked, nor stands in the way of sinners, nor sits in the seat of scoffers; but his delight is in the law of the LORD, and on his law he meditates day and night. He is like a tree planted by streams of water that yields its fruit in its season, and its leaf does not wither. In all that he does, he prospers.

PSALM 1:1-3

I'm ashamed to admit how many times I've seen the early-nineties film *Dumb and Dumber*. My teenage self found the crude, slapstick humor to be highly quotable and wildly hilarious. (To be clear, unless you're really into toilet-related gags, I do not recommend this movie.)

Despite its (many) faults, the movie's main characters, Lloyd and Harry, provide a marvelous picture for us today. As indicated by the film's title, the lesson here is obvious.

For better or worse, the people you're around *will* rub off on you. Be careful of the company you keep.

Our verses warn us right away whom to avoid specifically. The wicked, the sinners, the scoffers.

Though David elaborates in more detail about the fate of these in later verses, we get a quick glimpse into the life of the ungodly right here. We're warned not to walk in their counsel, stand in their ways, or sit in their seats. Rebellious, anxious, unsettled, they're all over the place—both literally and figuratively.

Contrast this with the one who delights in and meditates on God's Word. He is like a tree *planted*. Rooted. Solid. Held fast.

And not alone.

Undoubtedly, any gardener in that region with access to a water source would have taken full advantage of that wonderful resource. *Why plant one fruit tree, after all, when you can plant many fruit trees?*

God has likely surrounded us with an orchard of others. Godly women, firmly planted in the Word, desiring to see his name glorified, and just as in need of Christ-honoring friendships as we are.

Find these women. ASAP.

The company we keep is vital. I've seen it in my own life. I have wept many tears of joy over the godly women—older and younger—whom God has allowed me to walk through life with. Good friends and godly mentors are *critical* to our spiritual health.

The writer of Ecclesiastes confirms this wisdom: "Two are better than one, because they have a good reward for their toil" (4:9).

It's simple. More trees, more fruit.

Find a woman (or two) who loves Jesus, and plant yourself beside her. Grow together and watch God graciously and beautifully bless your life with fruit.

1. During trials, are you steadfast and solid, or does your faith waver? What does your reaction to difficulty reveal about how "planted" you are?

_____

_____

_____

_____

_____

2. Do you have a mentor, an accountability partner, or a godly woman who walks closely with you through life? If not, ask God to provide a woman you can ask to plant yourself beside and grow deeper with.

DAY 6

Blessed is the man who walks not in the counsel of the wicked, nor stands in the way of sinners, nor sits in the seat of scoffers; but his delight is in the law of the LORD, and on his law he meditates day and night. He is like a tree planted by streams of water that yields its fruit in its season, and its leaf does not wither. In all that he does, he prospers.   PSALM 1:1–3

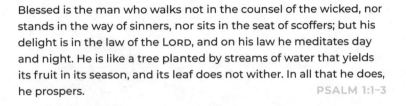

Take a few minutes today to journal and reflect on what God revealed to your heart through our verses this week. What did you learn about yourself or God? Is there a sin you need to confess and turn from or a truth you need to apply to your life? How have you been changed by meditating on this passage?

DAY 7

Blessed is the man who walks not in the counsel of the wicked, nor stands in the way of sinners, nor sits in the seat of scoffers; but his delight is in the law of the LORD, and on his law he meditates day and night. He is like a tree planted by streams of water that yields its fruit in its season, and its leaf does not wither. In all that he does, he prospers.

PSALM 1:1–3

Praying Scripture is a powerful practice that is simple, meaningful, and the perfect complement to your time of meditation on the Word. When we pray the Word, we can be sure we're praying God's will and therefore be confident we'll receive what we've asked for (see 1 John 5:15).

To close each week, spend some time praying our weekly Scripture back to the Lord. Feel free to use the suggested prayer as a guide, or simply pray as the Spirit leads. Then rest! God's promises are true. Let them satisfy and quiet your heart today.

 *Father God, I want to be a woman who is blessed by you! Please protect me from relationships that dishonor you and glorify sin. Teach me to delight in your Word and to meditate on it continually. Plant me beside godly people who are grounded in truth so that I am fruitful and strong in my faith. I pray you would cause me to prosper in all that I do for your glory and according to your perfect plans. Amen.*

Week 2

2 CORINTHIANS 5:21

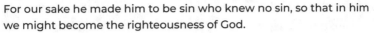

DAY 1

For our sake he made him to be sin who knew no sin, so that in him we might become the righteousness of God.

2 CORINTHIANS 5:21

Parenting, I've discovered, is a game of highs and lows.

One moment you're singing "Jesus Loves Me" with a cherub-faced toddler; the next you're pleading with them not to wipe their nose on the throw pillows.

Despite how the roles of parents seem to constantly teeter-totter from one extreme to the other, I'm learning that the primary calling of Christian parents is less about the extremes and more about hanging out in the middle.

As Paul David Tripp describes it, "Parenting is *ambassadorial* work from beginning to end."[1] We are the intermediaries, the ambassadors our King sends ahead to represent him to our children who do not yet know him.

Introducing them (and others) to God's love for them, expressed through Christ, is a job we must take extremely seriously.

The apostle Paul agreed. He wrote 2 Corinthians after a difficult season. Some in the church at Corinth had rebelled against his authority, and loyalties there had been painfully tested.

When Paul finally received word that many of his dissenters had repented, he wrote the Corinthians this letter.

Paul wasn't writing Scripture, as far as he knew. He was simply following up with faraway friends and sharing with them what God was teaching him (while under the inspiration of the Holy Spirit, of course). Yet Paul understood the seriousness of his role, the role of all of us who share his divine parentage.

He said, "We are ambassadors for Christ, as though God were making his plea through us. We plead with you on Christ's behalf, 'Be reconciled to God!'" (2 Cor. 5:20 NET).

Then he penned our Scripture for this week. A single sentence of such profound importance that biblical scholars largely agree it captures "the heart of the gospel."[2] It is, in short, the who, what, why, and how of our reconciliation with God.

We will spend a whole week on this one sentence. That may seem like a lot of time for just a few words, but what we are dealing with here is of eternal significance. It is critical that we know it, understand it, and believe it.

After all, to our children, our friends, our next-door neighbors, we are the ambassadors of the gospel. And these are the Words of Life.

1. Write 2 Corinthians 5:21 on a note card and work on memorizing it this week. Hiding the Word in your heart will prove to be a beneficial and long-lasting companion to your time of meditation.

2. Consider what it means to be an ambassador for Christ. If God is making his plea to others through us, how should this affect the way we view our current life roles (spouse, parent, daughter, sister, friend, employee)?

_____

_____

_____

_____

_____

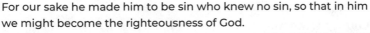

DAY 2

> For our sake he made him to be sin who knew no sin, so that in him we might become the righteousness of God.
>
> 2 CORINTHIANS 5:21

Martha wasn't trying to be funny, but she still made me laugh. She just caught me so off guard.

Here she was, a fellow student, speaking at a Christian event to Christian teenagers (myself included), and supergood, ultimate-Christian Martha said, totally straight-faced, "I have a black, black heart."

And I laughed. *Out loud.* It just struck me as so ridiculous.

Silly Martha! Martha was *perfect.* Martha never sinned. Martha did *not* have a black heart.

Did she?

Three tiny words from this week's verse—*for our sake*—tell us the truth about ourselves. My sixteen-year-old self did not understand it, but Martha did. She knew her true position before God—a fallen sinner in need of daily grace—and it's critical that we do too. Without this knowledge, we will never grasp what we've been given in Jesus.

The prophet Isaiah, calling out the Israelites for their rebelliousness, did not hold back. "But your iniquities have made a separation between you and your God. . . . Your lips have spoken lies; your tongue mutters wickedness" (Isa. 59:2–3).

Isaiah continued, but then casually switched pronouns to implicate himself too. "Therefore justice is far from us, and righteousness does not overtake us; we hope for light, and behold, darkness, and for brightness, but we walk in gloom" (v. 9).

The psalmist David agreed. "There is none who does good, not even one" (Ps. 14:3).

Martha and Isaiah and David were self-aware black hearts, fully mindful of their need for a Savior. Unlike high school me, who, despite my good behavior, perfect church attendance, and squeaky-clean reputation, had no idea the true condition of my heart.

Apart from Christ, my heart was (and is) black. Blackest of black.

It took one girl's humble confession in high school to alert me to the bad news . . . and the good news.

All is not lost. It never was.

Centuries before Jesus stepped foot on earth, Isaiah gave the Israelites (and all the rest of us) reason to hope: "Then his [God's] own arm brought him salvation. . . . 'A Redeemer will come to Zion'" (Isa. 59:16, 20).

For our sakes, Christ came and washed our black hearts clean.

God sent Jesus for us. For me. For you.

This is big, good news.

Praise him with me today.

---

1. What "color" is your heart? Take a moment to consider your heart's condition today. Are you relying on good behavior to make you right with God? Or do you feel your heart is too far gone to ever be right with him? What could be wrong with both of these lines of thinking?

_____

_____

_____

_____

2. If you have received the gift of God's grace, take a moment to praise him for your salvation. There is no better news we can be reminded of today.

DAY 3

For our sake he made him to be sin who knew no sin, so that in him we might become the righteousness of God.

2 CORINTHIANS 5:21

A word of advice: Do not let me choose paint colors.

Oh, how I wish I could go back a few years—mid–farmhouse remodel—and rescue myself from myself.

I painted the cabinets white, painted the shiplap white, and chose white tile for the bathroom floors. It just looked so clean and fresh and pretty on Pinterest, and Pinterest *never* lies.

Then we moved in.

I had always thought I kept a pretty tidy house, but the truth quickly came out.

The dried snot smears, muddy footprints, blobs of toothpaste, and spaghetti splatters could not lie against that pure white canvas. Our spots and stains were glaringly on display.

The pristine walls and floors that made those Pinterest houses look so gorgeous ended up instead just blatantly declaring the obvious in my house. We are filthy people.

It's a bit like looking at Jesus. Perfect, spotless, unstained Jesus. Next to him, all our junk, our sins large and small, are exposed for how dirty they really are. We are filthy people, stained with sin.

And perhaps the only thing worse than discovering the nastiness of our spots is realizing our own inability to do anything about it. There's no cleaning up this mess on our own. We're too soiled to even know where to start. Helpless and hopeless, we need someone to wash us clean.

Fortunately, God saw our mess coming and, in his incredible and unfathomable mercy, planned ahead.

Before the dirt beneath our feet was even a thing, he had already scheduled Jesus to die. "This Jesus, *delivered up according to the definite plan and foreknowledge of God,* you crucified and killed by the hands of lawless men" (Acts 2:23, italics mine).

On the cross, God took the holy canvas of his one and only Son and splattered our sins across him. God allowed Jesus's beauty and perfection to be marred by our filth so that we could be made clean at his expense.

Jesus's holiness is a big deal. Our sin is a big deal. And though Jesus knew no sin himself, God sent him as a stand-in for sin-stained us.

This alone is reason enough to stop everything right this moment and worship him.

Oh, Jesus, you are so, so good.

1. Reflect a moment on God's mercy toward you at the expense of his Son. What is your response? Are you unmoved or undone? Why?

_____

_____

_____

_____

_____

2. If you find that your spirit is not stirred by Jesus's sacrifice for you, ask the Holy Spirit right now to change your heart and to teach you to love and worship Jesus. This is a prayer God loves answering.

DAY 4

For our sake he made him to be sin who knew no sin, so that in him we might become the righteousness of God.

2 CORINTHIANS 5:21

I f I had to describe my relationship with God in one word, it would be this: *blueberries*.

Random, isn't it?

If we were having coffee, I'd tell you about the time God used a bag of blueberries to finally, absolutely convince me that he loved and cared for me. But since we're not, I'll tell you about the *second* time he did it.

My husband, Josh, and I were in the midst of a seemingly endless, exhausting season with one of our kids. Despite our prayers that our trials would end, they persisted.

So I changed tactics. I began to pray Psalm 5:12: "For you bless the righteous, O LORD, you cover him with favor as with a shield."

Father, I begged, *show us your favor. Remind us that you love us, even in the midst of this hard time.*

One morning, I reluctantly announced that our family wouldn't be able to do our beloved annual blueberry picking that year. We were just too busy. So, later that same day, when neighbors, unaware of our situation, surprised us with a bag of freshly picked blueberries, I laughed with joy. God *would* use blueberries to answer my prayer. *He loves us. He favors us.*

Once again, God had astonished me with his love. But that day, he went one step further and added in the gift of a new, life-changing realization: His kindness to me was *not because of me.*

I was dead in my sins (Eph. 2:1) until God swapped Jesus for me so that, as our verse this week tells us, I could "become the righteousness of God."

Become here means "to come into existence." As in, we go from unresponsive in death to full existence in righteousness. Because of Christ, God graciously credits us with this eternal right-standing before himself, a position otherwise held only by perfect, sinless, righteous Jesus.

And the incredible thing is, his kindness just keeps going.

Since God now looks on us as he looks on Christ, he generously and astonishingly continues to heap upon us the blessings deserved only by Christ.

Jesus's death for us yields God's favor for us.

Like blueberries sent to my door.

The righteous in Christ are covered by God's daily, undeserved personal favor.

Because of Jesus. Only because of Jesus.

---

1. Have you ever felt God's favor in a tangible, memorable way? Reflect on that moment. What does God's kindness reveal about his heart toward his children?

_____

_____

_____

2. If it's only because of Jesus that we "come into existence," how should this break our hearts for our unsaved friends? Pray today for someone you know to be brought to life in Christ.

_____

_____

_____

DAY 5

For our sake he made him to be sin who knew no sin, so that in him we might become the righteousness of God.

We recently had the privilege of watching two dear friends (as well as their young daughter) disrupt their comfortable lives to willingly dive into the messiness and frustration of our state's child welfare system. After a year of fostering two rambunctious toddlers, they have now adopted these precious brothers as their sons.

The boys, ages three and four, do not remember their lives before they came to their forever home. They call our friends "Mommy" and "Daddy" just as freely as their new older sister does. They rely on and enjoy the provisions from their mommy and daddy just as easily as their sister does. They know they are loved just as their sister does.

They have forgotten, mercifully, where they came from.

They take for granted, innocently, where they are now.

As I watched this process unfold, I realized that these little boys were not so very different from me.

I forget, quickly, where I came from. I take for granted, regularly, where I am now.

But it is so very important that we make ourselves remember.

From the beginning, God had appointed Jesus to stand in our place and take our much-deserved punishment.

At birth, we were black-hearted and dead in our sins (Ps. 51:5).

Immediately after we called on the name of the Lord to be saved, we "came into existence" in righteousness.

Then God looked on us—still bent toward sin but mercifully redeemed—and saw the righteousness of Christ, credited to us.

Now he lavishes on us the gifts fit only for One who is truly righteous. Fit only for Jesus.

We cannot overstate the importance of Jesus's work on the cross.

We must not take for granted that it was done for our sake nor allow it to become "old news" to us.

First thing in the morning, give yourself the truth of Jesus. What a life changer that could be.

Because, Jesus, you are *such a big deal.*

1. If you have never accepted Jesus Christ as your Savior and committed to following after him as Lord, the Bible is clear that all it takes to be saved is turning from your sins and receiving him in faith. "Because, if you confess with your mouth that Jesus is Lord and believe in your heart that God raised him from the dead, you will be saved" (Rom. 10:9). It's that simple. Christ died to give you life. Believe it, and let today be the glorious day you are made new.

2. You may have heard it said to "preach the gospel to yourself daily." What is the value of reminding yourself every morning (and frequently throughout the day) of the good news of Jesus?

DAY 6

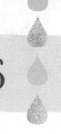

For our sake he made him to be sin who knew no sin, so that in him we might become the righteousness of God.

2 CORINTHIANS 5:21

Take a few minutes today to journal and reflect on what God revealed to your heart through our verse this week. What did you learn about yourself or God? Is there a sin you need to confess and turn from or a truth you need to apply to your life? How have you been changed by meditating on this passage?

DAY 7

For our sake he made him to be sin who knew no sin, so that in him we might become the righteousness of God.

2 CORINTHIANS 5:21

Close your week by praying the Word back to the Lord. Then rest! God's promises are true. Let them satisfy and quiet your heart today.

Lord Jesus, it was for my sake that you, the perfect One, were sent to bear the weight of sin. You stood in my place and swapped my black heart for the righteousness of God. Thank you for this gift that I don't deserve but will get to enjoy forever. Amen.

Week 3

1 THESSALONIANS
5:16–18

DAY 1

Rejoice always, pray without ceasing, give thanks in all circumstances; for this is the will of God in Christ Jesus for you.

1 THESSALONIANS 5:16–18

At approximately midnight on our first night home from the hospital with our fifth baby, our oldest baby vomited off the top bunk bed onto the wood floor below her.

She was eight.

She had eaten three hamburgers at dinner.

We *all* should have known better.

As I sopped up the horrific splattered mess, I was not rejoicing. Nor praying, nor thanking God for my circumstances. I was gagging.

Thank goodness my husband was there because I had to tag out. I woke him from his peaceful slumber with the happy news (*Guess who's on barf duty?!*) and then dragged my weary, angry, postpartum body back to bed.

Life, sometimes, is just hard.

Our verses this week are lovely in theory but oh so difficult to practice in a sometimes-just-hard life. I won't pretend otherwise.

Paul originally wrote these words to the new believers in first-century Thessalonica, where life, we can be sure, was hard. Especially for women.

With zero disposable diapers, very few rights of citizenship, and high rates of infant and maternal mortality, their lives must have been rife with frustrations and difficulty.

But Paul wasn't being insensitive to his audience, tacking on impractical theoretical commands to people already hard-pressed. Instead, we can be sure that, along with their new faith, the women who heard these words from Paul had also learned that, in Christ, they were new creations. Valuable, loved, and forgiven. This was good news.

"This is the will of God in Christ Jesus for you," he said. *This is what God has for you in Christ Jesus.*

It can be easy to glaze over while reading Scripture, especially when we've heard it all before, many times. But Paul's counsel here—new to his readers, ancient to us—has not aged a day. It is still just as relevant and important now as it was when he wrote it.

Life is hard, but there is always reason to rejoice *in Christ Jesus.*

Life is hard, but you can pray continually *in Christ Jesus.*

Life is hard, but there is always something to be thankful for *in Christ Jesus.*

Sometimes Scripture takes my breath away. *How had I not seen it before?* Everything circles back around to the same place. The same source.

Christ Jesus.

Joy, prayer, and gratitude are found fully in him.

Praise God. Life is hard, but Jesus is good.

1. Write 1 Thessalonians 5:16–18 on a note card and work on memorizing it this week. Hiding the Word in your heart will prove to be a beneficial and long-lasting companion to your time of meditation.

2. Read the verses again, thinking about what each part is saying. Does anything stand out to you that familiarity may have caused you to skip over before?

_____

_____

_____

_____

DAY 2

Rejoice always, pray without ceasing, give thanks in all circumstances; for this is the will of God in Christ Jesus for you.

1 THESSALONIANS 5:16–18

I'm just going to be honest here. The portion of our passage we'll talk about today is not a personal favorite. "Rejoice always."

I'm a pretty down-to-earth girl. Practical, reserved, unexcitable. The type of gal who can tamp down everyone else's excitability when necessary as well. (My superhero name in our house is, only half jokingly, "Captain Wet Blanket.")

I always just assumed that being joyful was a concept reserved for extroverts, cheerleader-types, and Santa Claus.

Imagine my surprise when I discovered very recently that I had been quite wrong.

Strong's Bible Dictionary defines *rejoice* as "to be calmly happy."[1]

Oh, how I love that.

Calmly happy: less a fickle, fleeting, circumstantial giddiness and more a quiet, steady gladness. Joyfulness at peace, if you will. I can get on board with that.

But still, practically speaking, what do we do with this command? Where is this constant, calm happiness in us supposed to come from?

David gives us some clues. He writes, very personally, "You make him [David] glad with the joy of your presence. For the king trusts in the LORD" (Ps. 21:6–7). And again in Psalm 28:7: "The LORD is my strength and my shield; in him my heart trusts . . . my heart exults, and with my song I give thanks to him."

Rejoicing always—calm, steady, peaceful happiness—results from a calm, steady, peaceful trust in God.

That explains how, as believers, we're able to be "sorrowful yet always rejoicing" (2 Cor. 6:10) or how the apostles were able to rejoice in persecution (Acts 5:41). It helps us understand why Paul can state that we are to "rejoice in hope" alongside a simultaneous command to be "patient in tribulation" (Rom. 12:12).

This command to rejoice always does not mean that we live like we're at a party that doesn't end. It *does* mean that we live like we have a hope that doesn't end.

Because we do.

We serve a God of hope.

Rejoicing always isn't some fluffy cliché or a fleeting feeling. It isn't a matter of personality. It *is* the calm, quiet happiness of a heart that trusts in its good and loving Father.

God's math is surprisingly simple sometimes: trust = joy.

And that's something we can rejoice in. Always.

1. Read this week's verses again. Do you find the idea of "rejoicing always" as intimidating as I do? How does the idea of "calm happiness" speak to your soul?

_____

_____

_____

2. What is your heart's condition today? Is it easy to rejoice? Or do you feel weary, worn out, or discouraged? Consider where your hopes lie. Are you trusting in God to bring you joy?

_____

_____

_____

DAY 3

Rejoice always, pray without ceasing, give thanks in all circumstances; for this is the will of God in Christ Jesus for you.

1 THESSALONIANS 5:16–18

Earlier in this letter, Paul encouraged the Thessalonians to "walk in a manner worthy of God" (1 Thess. 2:12). He gets pretty specific about what he means here, with instructions that may sound near impossible to our modern ears.

Pray unceasingly, he says. *Uninterruptedly.*

Who else finds this completely intimidating? Burdensome, even. *How could God possibly expect us to adhere to something so impractical?*

But the Holy Spirit is gentle. He reminds us of the truth: We have a kindhearted Father (Ps. 145:13) who issues his commands for our prosperity and success (Josh. 1:8), not to scare us away.

This isn't meant to be intimidating; it's meant to be an invitation.

Author Philip Yancey calls prayer "keeping company with God,"[1] which brings to mind a relationship so comfortable and familiar that both parties simply enjoy being in each other's presence, whether words are spoken or not.

John MacArthur helps by describing prayer as "spiritual breathing."[2] Just as our bodies are naturally compelled to breathe oxygen to live, so our lives and experiences around us should naturally compel us into God's presence. Every concern becomes a prayer of intercession, every blessing a reason to give thanks, every need rises up as a petition for his provision.

Burdens come in, prayers go out. In and out. As natural and as necessary as breathing. (Except when it's not.)

As with all things, prayerfulness takes practice. It is not easy. Fortunately (ironically!), when we struggle with prayerlessness, prayer is the first place we should turn.

As the worried father, who was so desperate to trust that Jesus could heal his son, cried out, "I believe; help my unbelief!" (Mark 9:24), so can we cry, "I want to pray; help my prayerlessness!"

This is a prayer we can trust our Father to always answer.

God Almighty welcomes us to keep company with him, to engage with him as often as we'd like in one-on-one, private conversation. We would be fools not to take him up on it.

Unceasing prayer is not a burden; it's a blessing.

---

1. Does praying without ceasing feel like an invitation or an added burden to your already busy life? How does it help to think of prayer as a conversation with a friend?

2. How does the command to pray without ceasing encourage you to be persistent in those long-term prayer requests that God has not yet answered? For the salvation of a friend or healing for a loved one, for example.

DAY 4

Rejoice always, pray without ceasing, give thanks in all circumstances; for this is the will of God in Christ Jesus for you.

1 THESSALONIANS 5:16–18

A line of note cards is taped above my kitchen sink. Despite them being faded, water-splotched, and mostly unreadable, I know by heart what's written on them. Scribbled with a verse or inspiring quote, those cards keep truth at eye level, staring me in the face every single day.

One of my most consulted (and most splotchy) cards bears a favorite quote I once heard. It says, "There is always something to complain about when your life is controlled by your feelings. There is much more to thank God for if your life is controlled by dwelling on his faithfulness, his love, and his mercy."

It's not an accident that these words reside in that particular spot. There is something about my seemingly endless kitchen duties that can draw entirely too many "feelings" out of me.

I don't feel like doing the dishes again.

I just feel off today.

I do not feel appreciated, and I definitely do not feel thankful.

(Yep. Kitchen feelings are *ugly*.)

I have learned (and am still learning) to beware "the feelings." They are untrustworthy, fickle, highly contagious to those around me, and originate dangerously in my heart, which we're told is "deceitful above all things and beyond cure" (Jer. 17:9 NIV).

The good news is, we don't have to let our feelings be in charge.

Paul writes in 2 Corinthians to "take every thought captive to obey Christ" (10:5).

Just as we seek to obey the Lord with our actions, so we should seek to obey him with our minds. Rerouting our thoughts to Christ, even when everything in us wants to complain, is an act of obedience and a solid first step toward thankfulness.

Why? Because it's hard to think about Christ without remembering what he's done for us. It's hard to remember what he's done without rejoicing. It's hard to rejoice without that joy turning into a prayer of thanksgiving.

Joy plus prayer yields thankfulness. (God's math strikes again!)

So Paul didn't casually link these three commands together. We can rejoice in our good, hope-giving Father. We can talk unceasingly to our ever-present, almighty Friend. And we find, in Christ, reason after reason to give thanks. No matter what our circumstances are.

And when "the feelings" do take over and I complain (again), I confess and am forgiven (again) by a kindhearted, gracious, astonishingly patient Savior.

No matter what our feelings are today, when we have Jesus, we always have something to give thanks for.

1. Kitchen duties are usually the least of our troubles. How does the command to give thanks apply in times of less frequent but far more substantial difficulties in our lives?

---

2. If you need a little refresher on why you can rejoice in Christ today, please read Ephesians 2:1–7. This is a wonderful go-to passage when you need the joy of your salvation restored.

DAY 5

Rejoice always, pray without ceasing, give thanks in all circumstances; for this is the will of God in Christ Jesus for you.

1 THESSALONIANS 5:16–18

First Thessalonians 5:16–18 is my laundry room truth.

(Notice a trend with me? I have a lot of household duties that I need a little biblical kick in the pants to get me through.)

This one's strategically positioned between the washer and dryer where I can see it when I begin to question the purpose of my life, which tends to happen most often while pairing socks. *Is this what I'm supposed to be doing, God? Should I be doing more? What is your will for me?*

It's a question we've probably all asked at some point. In some seasons, we ask because we need to make big, life-altering decisions. *Where should I go to college? Should I take the new job? Should I marry this guy?*

At other times, we ask because we just need a little confirmation for where we already are. *Am I doing what you want me to be doing, Lord? Am I on the right track?*

When we love God, we naturally want to do what he wants us to do. We want to be obedient to his will. But we also wouldn't mind knowing what that will is, right?

Thankfully, he's made it pretty clear.

"Rejoice always, pray without ceasing, give thanks in all circumstances; *for this is the will of God in Christ Jesus for you.*"

God's will is not a mystery we have to discern. It's not hidden or hard to determine.

God's will for us—no matter what career path we follow, who or if we marry, or what ministry opportunities we pursue—is to have a proper heart attitude before him.

Why?

Because of Jesus. This is the will of God *in Christ Jesus* for you.

Always, it comes back to Jesus.

His death on the cross means that sinners like us can enjoy right relationship with a holy God. It means that we can have life, and life to the fullest. It means that we have hope now and hope for the future.

And what naturally flows from the realization of this unmerited gift?

Rejoicing, prayer, and thankfulness.

There it is. Beautifully simple. God's will for us in Christ Jesus is that we have a heart that's calmly, prayerfully, thankfully happy in him—and that it shows.

Always.

1. Discerning God's will for our lives can be very stressful. Does it bring you peace today to know that he's actually made his will for you so clear and simple?

_____

_____

_____

2. In which of these three areas—rejoicing, prayer, or thankfulness—do you excel? Where do you have some room for improvement? What are some practical steps you can take to strengthen the areas where you're weak?

_____

_____

_____

_____

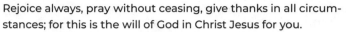

DAY 6

Rejoice always, pray without ceasing, give thanks in all circumstances; for this is the will of God in Christ Jesus for you.

1 THESSALONIANS 5:16–18

Take a few minutes today to journal and reflect on what God revealed to your heart through our verses this week. What did you learn about yourself or God? Is there a sin you need to confess and turn from or a truth you need to apply to your life? How have you been changed by meditating on this passage?

DAY 7

Rejoice always, pray without ceasing, give thanks in all circumstances; for this is the will of God in Christ Jesus for you.

1 THESSALONIANS 5:16–18

Close your week by praying the Word back to the Lord. Then rest! God's promises are true. Let them satisfy and quiet your heart today.

Father, help me today to rejoice always in Jesus and to remember that prayer is a privilege I am invited to enjoy continually. Please give me the grace to be thankful and to trust you no matter what my circumstances may be. Remind me that joy, prayer, and thankfulness are your will in Christ for me—and that your will is always perfect! Amen.

Week 4

2 CHRONICLES 20:12

We do not know what to do, but our eyes are on you.

We do not know what to do, but our eyes are on you.

DAY 1

We do not know what to do, but our eyes are on you.

2 CHRONICLES 20:12

If you were a churchgoing kid growing up in my generation, you may have taken part in a Sunday night children's choir program. These musical productions were usually reenacted Bible stories that included multiple original tunes and swell acting.

I remember one program's theme song particularly clearly. It was about the Old Testament king Jehoshaphat, and its chorus started like this: "He's fat, fat, Jehoshaphat. What a good, good king is he . . ."

(I was years-deep into adulthood before I came to the startling realization that nowhere in Scripture does it tell us that Jehoshaphat was portly. I guess "Jehoshaphat" was a challenging name for the songwriters to work with.)

I have *also* since discovered that one of the stories from his life—recorded in 2 Chronicles 20:1–23—is just phenomenal. For our study this week, we'll meditate on one key verse from that passage, but we'll approach it each day from within the context of the larger story.

As we'll learn, Jehoshaphat was not fat. But he was faith-full.

Jehoshaphat reigned over Judah about a century after King David. While many kings before and after him failed to follow God and, likewise, failed to lead their people to follow God, Jehoshaphat was different. "His heart was courageous in the ways of the Lord" (2 Chron. 17:6).

Yet when King Jehoshaphat was brought the dire news that a coalition of three enemy armies was approaching to attack his people, he was afraid (20:3). Judah was a tiny nation, easily outnumbered by this "great multitude" (v. 2) coming up against them. *They could not win this battle.*

Fear was understandable, but faith won out. Second Chronicles 20:3 tells us that King Jehoshaphat "set his face to seek the LORD."

I wonder how different my days would be if those words could also be said of me: *She set her face to seek the Lord.*

As we'll see this week, when we resolve to trust God like Jehoshaphat did, faithfully fixing our eyes on him alone, we may just get to witness his triumphant salvation on our behalf. And no matter how small or large those battles may be, *they will be fantastic to watch.*

Why wait? Let's set our faces to seek him *today.*

(While you're at it, take a few minutes to read ahead and enjoy all of 2 Chronicles 20:1–23 for yourself. I promise you won't be disappointed!)

1. Write 2 Chronicles 20:12 on a note card and work on memorizing it this week. Hiding the Word in your heart will prove to be a beneficial and long-lasting companion to your time of meditation.

2. Is there an area of your life that feels desperate right now? Are you fearful? Resolve to set your face to seek the Lord today. Fix your eyes and thoughts on Christ. He will be faithful.

_____

_____

_____

_____

DAY 2

We do not know what to do, but our eyes are on you.

We're in a super fun season right now at my church. There's no nursery or childcare offered on Sunday mornings, so the little darlings all join us in the service. Yippee.

Just a few weeks ago, our precious three-year-old tossed a marker box (markers I had brought to distract him) into the air—midsermon—with remarkable velocity.

It was distracting, all right.

Still, it was probably a relief to the many other frazzled parents sitting behind us. Even pastors' kids—and pastors' wives—struggle to keep it under control during church.

Which makes what happens next in our story even more amazing.

At the news of their enemies' imminent attack, King Jehoshaphat "proclaimed a fast throughout all Judah" (2 Chron. 20:3).

We're not told how long this fast lasted, but scholars believe it included men, women, and children. This could not have been easy but must have highlighted to everyone—children included—just how desperate the situation was. *Every* person in Judah was humbled in hunger before the Lord.

Jehoshaphat then stood in the temple and led his people in a powerful prayer (vv. 6–12), which he closed with the words that are our theme verse this week. It's a verse so rich and so simple and so applicable that I have cried it out to God myself over and over since I discovered it. "We do not know what to do, but our eyes are on you" (v. 12).

"Meanwhile all Judah stood before the Lord, with their little ones, their wives, and their children" (v. 13). What a testimony to these children! Not only did they, alongside their entire community, actively participate in setting their eyes upon the Lord, but they also would soon experience, alongside their entire community, God's incredible response.

James 4:10 says, "Humble yourselves before the Lord, and he will exalt you."

Whether it's in parenting or in marriage or in response to an unexpected difficulty, our desperation before our Father is a powerful witness to those watching—children and adults.

The more often we can cry out with Jehoshaphat, "I do not know what to do, but my eyes are on you!" the better.

Why? Because, as we'll see, God loves to bless the humble.

1. Consider the situations you're facing right now, and pray with Jehoshaphat, "I do not know what to do, but my eyes are on you." How does praying this prayer help release the weight of your personal battles?

_____

_____

_____

_____

_____

2. Do you consider yourself a humble person? Ask God to reveal any areas in your life where you might be a bit prideful, and seek his forgiveness for your self-reliance. Then joyfully receive his forgiveness. He loves to bless the humble!

DAY 3

We do not know what to do, but our eyes are on you.
2 CHRONICLES 20:12

My kids are finally old enough that hiking with them is *not* the most unpleasant experience in the world. Actually, it's almost enjoyable.

Recently, we trekked for hours among massive red rocks that inexplicably jut out of the Colorado soil. As my kids scrambled up and over and around those amazing landmasses, it was all I could do not to punctuate every moment with a mom-frantic "Be careful!" I tried hard to hold my tongue, but it wasn't easy.

I don't want them to get hurt, of course, but I really don't want to damage that innocent sense of fearlessness.

It's hard to get that back once it's lost.

After Judah's fasting and prayer, God's answer seemed to come at warp speed. The Spirit of the Lord came upon a man right there in the crowd, and he began to prophesy. "Do not be afraid and do not be dismayed at this great horde, for the battle is not yours but God's" (2 Chron. 20:15).

He told the troops to suit up yet finished powerfully with, "You will not need to fight in this battle. Stand firm, hold your position, and see the salvation of the LORD on your behalf" (v. 17).

We're told the people immediately fell down and began worshiping God. And who wouldn't? Can you imagine the joy they must have felt to be reassured so quickly and so decisively that God was with them?

Yet, as believers, are we not promised the same still today? Are we not commanded over and over in the Word to "fear not"? God has not changed, nor will he ever. The promises he spoke to Judah then apply to us now. Their manifestation will likely look different, but the promise holds true: "The battle is not yours but God's."

John Piper said, "The deepest root of Christian womanhood is hope in God. This hope in God yields fearlessness."[1]

Yes!

Fearlessness should mark us, sister in Christ. This doesn't mean that we will never be afraid but that when we set our eyes on him, our fears will bow down to something greater. Hope.

So stand firm, beloved. Hold your position.

God will (and does!) fight for you.

1. Some people are naturally fearless. Others seem born afraid. Where do you fall? Is fear a struggle for you? Why or why not?

2. We will face situations when a healthy fear is wise. But if fear characterizes us and heavily influences our decisions, it has crossed the line into sinful. What does fearfulness reveal about our true belief in God?

DAY 4

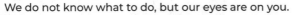

We do not know what to do, but our eyes are on you.

2 CHRONICLES 20:12

I was baiting my five-year-old's hook one afternoon when I heard his sweet little voice speak softly beside me.

"Dear Jesus," he prayed, "would you help me catch a fish? It would make me so happy."

I smiled at his innocent, earnest prayer request and helped him toss in his line. Moments later, he had his fish.

I love to think how it must have delighted God to answer my son. Rewarding the faith of his children is right in his wheelhouse, after all. It's kind of his thing.

The day of King Jehoshaphat's battle had arrived. The Israelites rose early, and Jehoshaphat addressed his troops. He said, "Believe in the LORD your God, and you will be established; believe his prophets, and you will succeed" (2 Chron. 20:20).

Then in what must have seemed like wild faith but wonky military strategy, we're told that Jehoshaphat "appointed those who were to sing to the LORD and praise him in holy attire" to go before the army and say, "Give thanks to the LORD, for his steadfast love endures forever" (v. 21).

Yep. The Israelites went marching into a humanly impossible military conflict against three fearsome, bloodthirsty armies, *and they sent the choir in first.*

To make matters more interesting, the choir sang a song of thanks. They were singing and praising and thanking God *before* they went into battle. Before they had witnessed what the outcome would be.

Theirs was an active, awesome faith. They believed God. And God was pleased.

Hebrews 11:6 tells us, "And without faith it is impossible to please him, for whoever would draw near to God must believe that he exists and that he rewards those who seek him."

Oh, he rewards, all right. Whether it's a fish caught by a preschooler or a victory in battle, God *loves*, *loves* to reward and rescue his children.

Psalm 18:19 says, "He brought me out into a broad place; he rescued me, because he delighted in me."

Is there any better news for us today? God delights in us. He delights in *you*. Rescuing and rewarding *you* pleases *him*.

Let's praise and thank him today for his love, even if the battle ahead of us still appears uncertain.

Our faith will become sight. It's a promise.

1. Do you believe God delights in you? Why or why not? Because of the blood of Christ, God looks upon us with the adoring eyes of a loving Father. Let your heart rejoice in that today.

2. Are you facing a battle today that feels unwinnable? How could embracing Jehoshaphat's method of thanking God in advance help in your situation?

DAY 5

We do not know what to do, but our eyes are on you.

2 CHRONICLES 20:12

If you read ahead in 2 Chronicles this week, you know two things: (1) the marvelous ending of this story and (2) that, sure enough, the fella who wrote the songs for my children's program so many years ago was taking some serious artistic license.

Jehoshaphat was not fat. But he was faith-full.

As soon as the Israelite choir opened their mouths to sing, "the LORD set an ambush against the men of Ammon, Moab, and Mount Seir, who had come against Judah" (20:22).

Suddenly, inexplicably, two of the armies turned against the third, "devoting them to destruction," then those two armies "all helped to destroy one another" (v. 23).

In the end, we're told not a single enemy troop escaped alive (v. 24).

All this happened while Judah simply stood back, sang, and watched.

God had not been kidding. The battle was his. Judah witnessed the salvation of the Lord without wielding a single weapon.

Why? Because they trusted God.

How? They fixed their eyes on him.

Jehoshaphat didn't panic or seek to control the situation himself when the future looked uncertain. Instead, he led his people in humbling themselves before the Lord. Together, they set aside any prideful self-confidence, admitted their need for help, and actively believed in God to rescue them.

"We do not know what to do, but our eyes are on you," Jehoshaphat had prayed. This little phrase—so easy to remember—opened the door to an astonishing display of the power of God.

Jehoshaphat expressed what should be the cry of the humbled heart all day, every day. And why not? The older I get, the more aware I am of how *little* I know, how painfully inadequate I am. I need the Lord's salvation on my behalf. Yesterday. Now. Tomorrow.

And this is good news! Because we are never, ever in a better position to watch God work than when we are humbled before him.

When the battle before us appears unwinnable, let us cry out with Jehoshaphat in humility. Then let's stand back, sing, and watch God do marvelous things.

After all, "Where does my help come from? My help comes from the Lord, the Maker of heaven and earth" (Ps. 121:1–2 NIV).

1. Why is being desperate before God—with nowhere else to turn— a good place to be? Intellectually, we may believe that it is, but how do you respond in actual desperate circumstances? Does your faith need some work in this area?

_____

_____

_____

_____

_____

_____

_____

2. Think back on a time in your life when God astonished you with his provision. Reflect on it and tell someone else about it today.

DAY 6

We do not know what to do, but our eyes are on you.

2 CHRONICLES 20:12

Take a few minutes today to journal and reflect on what God revealed to your heart through our verse this week. What did you learn about yourself or God? Is there a sin you need to confess and turn from or a truth you need to apply to your life? How have you been changed by meditating on this passage?

DAY 7

We do not know what to do, but our eyes are on you.

2 CHRONICLES 20:12

Close your week by praying the Word back to the Lord. Then rest! God's promises are true. Let them satisfy and quiet your heart today.

Heavenly Father, when circumstances in my life appear unwinnable, remind my heart that you are my help. When I don't know what to do, help me to keep my eyes on you. The battles I face are not mine but yours, Father. Amen.

Week 5

JOHN 15:5

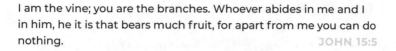

DAY 1

I am the vine; you are the branches. Whoever abides in me and I in him, he it is that bears much fruit, for apart from me you can do nothing.

JOHN 15:5

Here's a fun fact I learned early in marriage: submitting stinks. Or at least, I stink at submitting.

Despite knowing and believing that a wife submitting to her husband is good and biblical, despite being married to a kind and godly man, I did not realize how much it would rile me to have to submit to him.

Yet it's helped me greatly (and may help fellow reluctant submitters like me) to remember that God does not ask something of us that he wasn't willing to first do himself.

Our verse this week is found tucked inside John 15, which uses the extended metaphor of tending grapevines to describe the relationship between God the Father (the vinedresser), Jesus (the vine), and us (the branches).

It begins with Jesus's words, "I am the vine."

There are seven "I am" statements in the book of John[1]—places where Jesus boldly and purposefully declared his own divinity by quoting God when he revealed his name to Moses at the burning bush: "I AM WHO I AM" (Exod. 3:14).

Yet, immediately following the powerful "I am" in our verse, Jesus further shocks with a statement of definitive humility. "I am *the vine*." And vines, of course, are at the mercy of their vinedressers.

In four short words, Jesus was declaring himself both to be God and to be in submission to God. In fact, obedience to his Father's will was

Jesus's ultimate motivation. He told his disciples, "My food is to do the will of him who sent me and to accomplish his work" (John 4:34).

So why would Jesus submit? And what does it have to do with us?

Paul explains, "Jesus . . . who *for the joy that was set before him* endured the cross" (Heb. 12:2, italics mine). Jesus submitted, even unto death, because Jesus was choosing joy.

His obedience to the Father's will, his willingness to be the vine in the Great Vinedresser's hand, is a light to our path.

Seeking joy? he says. Do like I do: obey the Father.

We may never consider submission *enjoyable*, but it is an important part of our journey if our desired destination is joy.

Where Jesus leads the way, it's always wise to follow.

1. Write John 15:5 on a note card and work on memorizing it this week. Hiding the Word in your heart will prove to be a beneficial and long-lasting companion to your time of meditation.

2. If Jesus was humble and obedient, what does it mean for you? Are you submissive to the authorities in your life? If improvement is needed, ask the Lord to show you where and how.

DAY 2

I am the vine; you are the branches. Whoever abides in me and I in him, he it is that bears much fruit, for apart from me you can do nothing.
JOHN 15:5

There was a season in my college years during which I became a statistic.

I stopped reading my Bible. I skipped chapel as often as possible. I distanced myself from other believers and ignored the Holy Spirit's conviction of my sin. I strayed.

And while this path was of my choosing, I remember that time in my life as desperately disconnected and sad. I had become uninterested in my faith, and though I wouldn't have admitted it, as a result, I flat-out *withered*.

And Jesus tells us flat-out *why*.

We are the branches. Branches are connected to a vine and are reliant on the vine for all they need. The vine alone is their source of nourishment. Their lives literally depend on it.

The analogy here is easy to see. Jesus is our source. If we disconnect from him, out of busyness or rebellion or uninterest, we *will* begin to wither, and we *definitely* won't be fruitful.

We are either ignorant or arrogant if we think we can do life without him. Because if we don't find our source of life in Christ, we will seek to find our nourishment through something else.

We've heard it said that everyone worships something. If that something is not God, we will foolishly bow down to something else.

Our beauty. Our careers. Our kids. Shopping. Working out. Our followers. Fame.

Caring about these things is not necessarily sinful, but worshiping them is. And when we find ourselves asking them to nourish us, we will wither. No way around it.

In college, I was trying to find life through my relationship with a guy. But he could not sustain me. It wasn't his fault; he was just another branch, not the vine. He could not give me what I needed.

Only Jesus could.

Paul says, "And my God will supply every need of yours according to his riches in glory in Christ Jesus" (Phil. 4:19). He alone is worthy of worship because he alone is rich in the nourishment we need for life. For abundance. Joy. Hope.

Let's repent today if we've sought life through any other source.

Jesus, keep us dependent on you.

Only you are rich enough to supply all we need.

1 · Where have you sought to find life apart from Christ, either now or in the past? What is it about that particular thing that draws you to it?

_____

_____

_____

2 · What practical steps can you take today to step away from the things you're particularly tempted to worship? How does it help to know that God is rich in all you need?

_____

_____

_____

DAY 3

I am the vine; you are the branches. Whoever abides in me and I
in him, he it is that bears much fruit, for apart from me you can do
nothing.
JOHN 15:5

I f you have kids, you may be familiar with their occasional "lean in"
approach to affection.

I come seeking a sweet good-night kiss; they lean toward me,
forehead first, to receive it. I want a warm, full bear hug; they offer only
a stiff side hug. What is that about? I am their mom. I birthed, nursed,
bathed, and wiped them . . . their "leans" earn them nothing but an of-
fended parent.

Yet "lean in" has become a cultural catchphrase, especially in Christian
circles. We're told to "lean in" to our grief. "Lean in" to hard conversa-
tions. Or, most woefully, I think, to "lean in" to Jesus.

If all we do is lean in, we are missing out.

Jesus says in our verse we are to abide in him, and he will abide in us.
Abide means "to stay, remain, reside."

Spatially, abiding puts us "in Christ." This is no stiff side hug with
Jesus. It's going deep with him. Planting our lives firmly inside his will.
Obeying his commands. Trusting our every moment to the riches of
his grace. Clinging furiously and fearlessly to the promises of his Word.
Knowing that faith "in Christ" alone is our source of life, strength, and joy.

So how do we do it? How do we abide in him?

Brother Lawrence, a humble dishwasher in a French monastery in
the 1600s, is famous for his unusually intimate relationship with God.

He wrote, "I keep my attention on God in a simple, loving way. This
is my soul's secret experience of the actual, unceasing presence of God.
. . . Do not forget Him! Think of Him often; adore Him ceaselessly; live

and die with Him. That is the real business of a Christian; in a word, it is our profession."[1]

Leaning in is easy. It requires little from us. Abiding is meant to be a serious, life-altering commitment. It necessitates packing up everything—our hopes, plans, dreams, and desires—and relocating them in Christ.

Is it worth it?

Jesus seemed to think so. "These things I have spoken to you, that my joy may be in you, and that your joy may be full" (John 15:11).

There it is again. Joy.

Yes, friend, abiding is absolutely worth it.

1. Brother Lawrence said abiding in Christ should be the "real business" of our lives. What practices or habits can you develop in your daily life that will help make it your business to abide in Christ?

_____

_____

_____

_____

2. Read Ephesians 1:3–14. Underline in your Bible every time Paul uses words like "in Christ," "in him," or "through Jesus." My Bible labels this passage "Spiritual Blessings in Christ." Read through it, and let these blessings refresh and restore your soul in Christ today.

DAY 4

I am the vine; you are the branches. Whoever abides in me and I
in him, he it is that bears much fruit, for apart from me you can do
nothing.

There is a common assumption that because my husband, kids, and I live on a farm, we must be good gardeners. It's understandable.

With all that sunny space, we really ought to be able to enjoy delicious homegrown okra in the summer and our own canned tomatoes in the winter.

Except we don't. Because we're terrible.

We can grow children and chickens and the occasional cow, but not much else. Despite our best efforts, we don't bear much *actual* fruit.

Fortunately for us, Jesus isn't concerned with a bumper crop of cucumbers. But in the grander and much more important scope of Christianity, fruitfulness is a very big deal to him.

Paul says it's our primary purpose. We were "created in Christ Jesus for good works" (Eph. 2:10). James agreed: "So also faith by itself, if it does not have works, is dead" (James 2:17).

Our fruit will mark us as true believers.

Though we know that salvation comes through faith alone and works cannot produce it (see Eph. 2:8–9), true salvation *will* produce fruit that will be for God's glory and exclusive to the follower of Christ.

The *Pillar New Testament Commentary* tells us that throughout John 15, "'fruit' in the vine imagery represents everything that is the product of effective prayer in Jesus' name, including obedience to Jesus' commands (v. 10), experience of Jesus' joy (v. 11), love for one another (v. 12) and witness to the world (vv. 16, 27)."[1]

An effective prayer life, radical obedience, joyfulness, the ability and desire to love and share Christ with our neighbors . . . it's all dependent on our dependence on him.

Just as a branch cannot bear fruit if it's not connected to its vine, so we as believers will not experience the exciting and life-changing work that can be done through us unless we abide in Christ.

If we're frustrated by the limited fruit in our lives, it's okay. God is exceedingly patient. He knows that, for the faithful believer, bearing good fruit should, quite literally, take a lifetime. "The righteous flourish like the palm tree. . . . They still bear fruit in old age; they are ever full of sap and green, to declare that the LORD is upright" (Ps. 92:12, 14–15).

Our source is Christ. If we abide in him, and make abiding our main concern, fruit *will* grow.

Not for our glory, but for Christ's alone.

1. Which of the "fruits" discussed in John 15 are you rich in? Which areas need work? Admit your need to Christ today and trust him to lead you in any steps you may need to take to increase your fruitfulness.

_____

_____

_____

2. Read James 2:14–26. How does Abraham's example give a better understanding of how faith and good works go hand in hand?

_____

_____

_____

DAY 5

I am the vine; you are the branches. Whoever abides in me and I in him, he it is that bears much fruit, for apart from me you can do nothing.

Remember learning in school about similes and metaphors and analogies?

Me neither.

But it must have happened somewhere around the third grade.

I was complaining to my husband about the never-ending nature of cleaning one afternoon, and to emphasize the utter unfairness of my plight, I whined, "I've already straightened this living room three hundred times today."

To that, my nine-year-old helpfully chimed in from nearby, "Mom, that's hyperbole."

Touché.

In case your knowledge of figures of speech is as rusty as mine, *hyperbole* is the intentional use of exaggeration to make a point.

Yes, I was exaggerating. No, Jesus is not.

His claim in our passage is strong: "Apart from me you can do nothing." *Nothing? Really? Surely he doesn't mean that.*

Yet the *New American Commentary* emphasizes, "The radicality of John's Gospel should not be missed by familiarity with its words. Nothing is 'not something' in the judgment of Jesus. It's still nothing."[1]

It's easy to justify Jesus's words as applying to unbelievers. Sure, they may succeed financially, dazzle socially, and spend their days climbing their respective ladders straight up to worldly rewards, but unless their endeavors are done through Christ and in Christ and for Christ, they are counted as nothing, eternally speaking.

But we believers must listen up as well. Jesus was talking to us too.

Consider Paul's words about ministry in 1 Corinthians: "According to the grace of God given to me, like a skilled master builder I laid a foundation. . . . Let each one take care how he builds upon it. For no one can lay a foundation other than that which is laid, which is Jesus Christ" (3:10–11).

It does not matter how grand our accomplishments for God are or how well-meaning our intentions, if our day-to-day, moment-by-moment posture is not that of abiding in Christ and building upon his foundation, any fruit we produce will not survive the testing fires of eternity (vv. 12–15).

This is a hard truth, yet with so much at stake, it bears repeating and remembering.

We must abide in Christ and he in us. Apart from him we can do nothing.

And that's no exaggeration.

1. Which areas of your life are bearing eternal fruit? Which are not? What can you do to remedy any fruit-deficient trouble spots?

_____

_____

_____

2. Christ calls us to abide for our own good. What do we gain through abiding in Christ? Alternately, what do we miss out on if we don't?

_____

_____

_____

DAY 6

I am the vine; you are the branches. Whoever abides in me and I in him, he it is that bears much fruit, for apart from me you can do nothing.

JOHN 15:5

Take a few minutes today to journal and reflect on what God revealed to your heart through our verse this week. What did you learn about yourself or God? Is there a sin you need to confess and turn from or a truth you need to apply to your life? How have you been changed by meditating on this passage?

DAY 7

I am the vine; you are the branches. Whoever abides in me and I
in him, he it is that bears much fruit, for apart from me you can do
nothing.
JOHN 15:5

*Close your week by praying the Word back to the Lord. Then rest! God's
promises are true. Let them satisfy and quiet your heart today.*

 *you were the humble vine, joyfully submitting to
God. Help me, Lord, to make it my business to be like you—
abiding in you, dependent upon you. Bear fruit in me that
will last and will bring you glory. Apart from you, Jesus, I
can do nothing. Amen.*

Week 6

NAHUM 1:7

DAY 1

The LORD is good, a stronghold in the day of trouble; he knows those who take refuge in him.   NAHUM 1:7

Years ago, while I was wading back into the faith I had strayed from, a mentor recommended I read a book by A. W. Tozer. I dove in, and truth overcame me.

Tozer said, "What comes into our minds when we think about God is the most important thing about us."[1]

My eyes were opened. My rebellion, my lack of trust in God, and my weak faith all could be linked to erroneous beliefs about my Father. For once, it was such a relief to be wrong.

Our verse this week comes from Nahum, a short, mostly bleak book.

Nahum prophesied that judgment was coming for Nineveh, the capital city of Assyria, one of Israel's most dreaded enemies. For generations, the Assyrians had terrorized other nations. The Israelites had suffered deeply at their hands.

God had given the Assyrians opportunities to change. Just a century earlier, he had sent Jonah to them to preach repentance. Though they embraced Jonah's message initially, their newfound faith was short-lived.

Now Nahum brought God's Word to the Israelites. There were no more chances for the Assyrians. God, Nahum promised, "will make a complete end of the adversaries" (Nah. 1:8).

Though Nahum's prophecy surely brought rejoicing in Israel, there must have been many prior years of wondering where God was. *Why doesn't he act? How can he allow this evil?*

Is God really good?

It's a question we all have likely asked. I certainly have. Some days I still do.

Which is why it is so critical not just that we *know* our verse this week but that we *believe* it.

Believing that the Lord is good and that we are safe in him is foundational to our faith.

We may believe that God created us, even that he loves us, but if we don't believe he is also good, we will inevitably struggle to trust him. We will doubt his methods and question his discipline. We will wonder if following him is worth it.

And, have no doubt, this is exactly what the enemy wants us to do.

So what *is* God like? Is he good?

Let's seek the answers together this week. It is, I believe, one of the most important things we can do.

1. Write Nahum 1:7 on a note card and work on memorizing it this week. Hiding the Word in your heart will prove to be a beneficial and long-lasting companion to your time of meditation.

2. Do you believe God is good? Do you believe he's good no matter your circumstances? Take a moment and think of a time when you've seen the goodness of God in your own life, especially during a difficult time.

_____

_____

_____

_____

DAY 2

The LORD is good, a stronghold in the day of trouble; he knows those who take refuge in him.   NAHUM 1:7

Yesterday was one of those days.

Unexpected overnight guests were coming. The washing machine backed up and flooded the laundry room. I needed to have a tricky and unpleasant conversation with a health-care provider. I felt unprepared, out of control, and frustrated.

But I had our verse on my mind. Though my response to my troubles was not perfect, I was able to say to my children, as they watched me sop up sudsy water while still in my pajamas, "This is a mercy, kids. Somehow, this is God being good to us."

Sometimes, we just have to preach it, even when the sermon is mostly meant for ourselves.

Though Nahum foretold of Assyria's coming destruction, scholars believe their end likely still didn't come until some fifteen to forty-five years later. Israel had been promised that the Lord would deliver wrath on their enemies, yet their wait continued. Why?

Short, disappointing answer? I don't know.

But I do know this: Waiting as a means of teaching his children to trust is a method near and dear to God's heart. So many of the stories we read in Scripture involve long periods of waiting. Abraham waited for an heir. Joseph waited in prison. Moses and the Israelites waited to enter the promised land.

God loves to give us opportunities to wait *and wait well*.

Then, in his goodness, at just the right time, he *also* loves to rescue and reward.

King David, in the midst of his many personal troubles, was the ultimate self-preacher. "I believe that I shall look upon the goodness of the Lord in the land of the living! Wait for the Lord; be strong, and let your heart take courage; wait for the Lord!" (Ps. 27:13–14).

You just wait, he told his heart. *God will be good.*

God's goodness is not just a theological doctrine to be memorized; it is a truth we can expect and anticipate. We *will* see the goodness of the Lord in the land of the living. We *will* be recipients of his mercy. We *will* benefit from his grace.

Stake a claim in this truth. Stand upon it. And when you start to forget, preach it to yourself. No matter how long we have to wait, we *will* see the goodness of the Lord.

The Lord is too good and too kind for our waiting to ever be wasted.

---

1. In what areas of your life are you waiting on God today? How do Nahum 1:7 and Psalm 27:13–14 comfort you as you wait?

_____

_____

_____

_____

2. How can you seek to honor and glorify God while you wait? What does it look like to wait well?

_____

_____

_____

The LORD is good, a stronghold in the day of trouble; he knows those who take refuge in him.   NAHUM 1:7

While speaking at a women's event one January, I presented a personal resolution I had made for the new year. Rather than fearing my unknown future, I would anticipate seeing the goodness of God that year. I encouraged the women to join me in my experiment. "We will see God be good," I said. "Let's wait expectantly together."

Eleven months later, at another speaking event, I summarized my year.

In short, it was awful. Fraught with conflict, setbacks, and uncomfortable life change, nothing about that year had been "good." Yet I learned lessons about God over those months that I could only have learned through difficulty.

That year was trouble, but the Lord had held me close. Sure enough, I saw *him* be good.

The experiment was a success.

Nestled inside the doom and gloom of Nahum, God has planted this wonderful promise for his people: "The Lord is good, a stronghold in the day of trouble" (1:7).

These two promises go so hand in hand—are so closely related—that they are presented as a parallel thought. Just as assuredly as we find God is good, we will find troubles. Yet God is our safe place within them, *even as it is God who allows the storm in the first place.*

Oh my, there is such mystery here. How can this be?

Lamentations 3:31–33 gives us a peek into God's inscrutable ways: "For the Lord will not cast off forever, but, though he cause grief, he will have compassion according to the abundance of his steadfast love; for he does not afflict from his heart or grieve the children of men."

God's heart toward us is kind, compassionate, and abundantly good. He is not happy when we suffer. Yet when he allows the day of trouble to come, he promises to be our refuge. And it's there we find compassion and comfort in his steadfast love.

God, in his unfathomable wisdom, is both the creator of the storm and our stronghold within it. We may never fully understand this, but that does not make it any less true.

No, we are not guaranteed a life free from danger, sister, but we *are* guaranteed a safe and secure stronghold within the storm.

1 · How does the truth that God is both the creator of the storm and our stronghold within it sit with you? Hosea 6:1 says, "Come, let us return to the Lord; for he has torn us, that he may heal us; he has struck us down, and he will bind us up." What additional insight does this verse provide about God's good purposes for our pain?

_____

_____

_____

_____

2 · Colossians 3:3 says, "For you have died, and your life is hidden with Christ in God." What does it mean to you that you are hidden with Christ in God?

_____

_____

_____

DAY 4

The LORD is good, a stronghold in the day of trouble; he knows those who take refuge in him.   NAHUM 1:7

I don't fly often, but when I do, I always find myself looking out the window and marveling at how small life below me suddenly looks. Tiny little cars hurry on tiny little roads, driven by tiny little drivers scurrying to get wherever they're going. From up high, all that rushing about looks, well, silly.

We're so insignificant, I find myself thinking. *We feel big and important, but in comparison to the world around us, we're minuscule. Just one small soul in a sea of billions . . .*

Yes, that sounds like I have a terribly low view of humankind. And I might, were it not for what God has to say about us instead.

"He knows those who take refuge in him" (Nah. 1:7).

The word *knows* here is translated "cares for" in the NIV Bible. It is a lovely and true thought, of course, that God cares for us. But *knows* has a different feel to it, doesn't it? It sits a bit heavier.

Jesus echoed this language in his famous conversation with the Pharisees. "I am the good shepherd" (John 10:11), he told them. "My sheep hear my voice, and I know them, and they follow me" (v. 27).

The sheep hear the shepherd and follow because he is familiar to them. They recognize him by a physical quality—his voice. But the shepherd is different; he *knows* his sheep. Just as God knew us before we were formed in the womb (Ps. 139:13), just as he is keenly aware of something as trivial as the number of hairs on our heads (Matt. 10:30), *he knows our hearts and all that is in them.*

The deepest parts of who we are, the parts we never reveal to others or may not even understand about ourselves, are held, precious and safe, in God's fathomless treasury of wisdom. There is nothing about us that is hidden from him. We. Are. Known.

The enemy will try to convince us otherwise, of course, but Nahum assures us it's true. Second Timothy backs it up: "But God's firm foundation stands, bearing this seal: 'The Lord knows those who are his'" (2:19).

We are fully known and *still* so deeply loved, beloved.

Praise God.

1. How does the idea that God, your Creator, knows and loves you fully and completely comfort your heart today? How does believing this truth free you from hiding yourself and your struggles from God? From others?

_____

_____

_____

_____

_____

2. I love the song "Known" by Tauren Wells. Find a way to listen to it today, and let this wonderful truth wash over you in worship.

DAY 5

The LORD is good, a stronghold in the day of trouble; he knows those who take refuge in him.

NAHUM 1:7

At the time of this writing, we are in the middle of the COVID-19 pandemic.

We are already months in, but since the state where I live has not yet peaked, predictions suggest it may still last many more months.

Today, this news hits me hard, and I feel I cannot bear up under the weight of it. *How long, O Lord?* I feel almost despair.

I've reached out to my pray-ers to pray for me. Pray I will trust the Lord, I ask. Pray I will *cling* to the truth.

This is where our faith becomes real, sister. This is where it moves from theology to action. What do we do when the foundations are shaken? How do we respond when God does not seem to be good? Will we still trust in him?

Amazingly, this wondering and questioning is what God wants. *Because it's time*, he says. *It's time to decide. Who do you believe I am?* he asks. *Do you believe that I am good, a stronghold in the day of trouble? That I know you?*

Child, do you trust me?

I love that the American Sign Language sign for *trust* is a motion that resembles both hands grabbing on to a thick rope.

Yes.

When we question, we grab on to the answers he gives in his Word. We cling to the truths in Scripture like our lives depend on it. *Because they do.*

What happens when we let go of the rope? We fall.

Our dear King David, who knew so many troubles, was pretty darn clingy in a very good way. "Incline your ear to me," he cried to God. "Rescue me speedily! Be a rock of refuge for me, a strong fortress to save me!" (Ps. 31:2).

Then, in faith, David clung. "But I trust you, O Lord; I say, 'You are my God.' My times are in your hand" (vv. 14–15).

This is the kind of faith that pleases the heart of our Father.

How do we know? Listen to God's answer: "Because he holds fast to me in love, I will deliver him; I will protect him, because he knows my name" (91:14).

Today, join with me. Let's grab on to Nahum 1:7 and verses like it and *hold fast*. Our very faith depends on it.

1. What circumstances are weighing heavy on you today? What truth about God will you choose to cling to today to comfort and quiet your anxious heart?

2. Read and enjoy Psalm 91. How does this passage reinforce what we've talked about this week?

DAY 6

The LORD is good, a stronghold in the day of trouble; he knows those who take refuge in him.   NAHUM 1:7

Take a few minutes today to journal and reflect on what God revealed to your heart through our verse this week. What did you learn about yourself or God? Is there a sin you need to confess and turn from or a truth you need to apply to your life? How have you been changed by meditating on this passage?

DAY 7

The LORD is good, a stronghold in the day of trouble; he knows those who take refuge in him.

NAHUM 1:7

Close your week by praying the Word back to the Lord. Then rest! God's promises are true. Let them satisfy and quiet your heart today.

Lord, you are perfectly, faithfully good. You are my safe, strong place in these days of trouble. You love it when I come running to you because I am yours, and you know me fully and completely. Give me the grace, Jesus, to believe and hold fast to this deep and wonderful truth. Amen.

Week 7

1 PETER 3:3–4

DAY 1

Do not let your adorning be external—the braiding of hair and the putting on of gold jewelry, or the clothing you wear—but let your adorning be the hidden person of the heart with the imperishable beauty of a gentle and quiet spirit, which in God's sight is very precious.

1 PETER 3:3-4

I'm usually excited about the verses God leads me to reflect on. This week, not so much.

We've heard it all before, Lord, I whined. *It's the stereotypical passage for women. What could I possibly teach?*

But I plowed on—and then was reminded that our verses are found smack dab in the middle of a passage on marriage. *These are verses about submission.*

Please no, Jesus.

But Jesus said, "Yep," and then allowed me to see the condition of my own sin-sick heart last week in such a providential and devastating way that I knew why.

Ah, I am not here to teach. I am here to learn.

Our verses come from a letter Peter wrote most likely to gentile believers. They wouldn't have grown up in the Jewish faith with God's laws regarding marriage to guide them, so the information Peter was giving them was new. They were here to learn too.

Peter explained that submission is *not* the idea of a husband lording over his wife, as husbands and wives are equal in Christ, coheirs in grace (1 Pet. 3:7). Rather, submission is a beautiful calling to all believers to teach us to hope in God.

For women specifically, it seems to have less to do with a wife's position in relation to her husband than it does her heart's position in relation to its Father.

Therefore, this passage isn't just for married women but for any woman who calls herself a child of God.

Forgo the temporary beauty of external adornments, Peter urges, and focus instead on the hidden person of the heart, a person of unfading beauty and a gentle and quiet spirit. A person precious to the God she hopes in.

If you're not so sure you're up to it this week—maybe, like me, you recognize how short you fall of this passage—we can take that as a good sign. The Lord has room to work. "So we do not lose heart. Though our outer self is wasting away, our inner self is being renewed day by day" (2 Cor. 4:16).

Renew us, Lord. Teach us by your Word.

We're in this together. Here to learn.

1. Write 1 Peter 3:3-4 on a note card and work on memorizing it this week. Hiding the Word in your heart will prove to be a beneficial and long-lasting companion to your time of meditation.

2. What is your reaction to the word *submission*? Think about it in terms of marriage if you're married, or in relation to your boss, your parents, even God. Pray with me that God would open our eyes to whatever he wants to teach us this week.

DAY 2

Do not let your adorning be external—the braiding of hair and the putting on of gold jewelry, or the clothing you wear—but let your adorning be the hidden person of the heart with the imperishable beauty of a gentle and quiet spirit, which in God's sight is very precious.

1 PETER 3:3-4

I have the sweetest gal who does my hair. She loves the Lord, loves me, and suffers through my impossibly thick mane with a smile on her face. She always shoots me straight too. Until a few weeks ago.

At a recent appointment, she casually mentioned my "clear" hairs, which, she noted, were becoming more numerous.

"Clear?" I asked, unfamiliar with the term.

"Yeah, you know." She lowered her voice. "*Clear.*"

I laughed. Hard.

I'm not at all opposed to covering my gray—er, clear—hairs, but I'm well aware it's a losing battle. My youth is fading, and my hair is going with it.

When Peter addressed external adornments here, it was not to condemn all efforts toward physical beauty but to remind us that something more important is at stake: "the hidden person of our hearts." Why?

Because she matters deeply to the Lord.

When God sent Samuel to anoint a new king for Israel from among Jesse's sons, Samuel assumed God would choose the oldest and most handsome for the job. But God didn't. Instead, he said, "Do not look on his appearance. . . . For the LORD sees not as man sees: man looks on the outward appearance, but the LORD looks on the heart" (1 Sam. 16:7).

We must not let familiarity with these words blind us to their real-life implications.

There is no hiding behind makeup or fashion, right behavior or good works. The hidden person of the heart is the woman in us who stands before the Lord, exposed, uncovered, and known as she truly is.

What God sees in our hearts matters above all else to him. It should matter above all else to us too. Our hidden persons are our most valuable asset, both now and for eternity.

No matter how hard we try to prevent it, our earthly bodies will gray, fade, and wear out, but our hearts—known, loved, and precious to God—will not. It is no coincidence Peter calls their beauty "imperishable."

We would do well to follow King Solomon's wise advice: "Above all else, guard your heart, for everything you do flows from it" (Prov. 4:23 NIV).

Lord, teach us to rightly value our hidden persons like you do!

1. Have you placed an unhealthy emphasis on your outward appearance? If so, how? Ask God to help you find the balance of caring for your body—his temple—without neglecting your heart, your most precious commodity!

2. What do you think Solomon meant when he said to "guard your heart"? What should you guard it from? Why is this so important?

DAY 3

Do not let your adorning be external—the braiding of hair and the putting on of gold jewelry, or the clothing you wear—but let your adorning be the hidden person of the heart with the imperishable beauty of a gentle and quiet spirit, which in God's sight is very precious.

1 PETER 3:3–4

I wish I could have a do-over of last week.

My husband is pursuing a new business venture, so I had the wonderful opportunity to be his biggest cheerleader. Instead, I "submitted" to his decision with gritted teeth and a bitter heart.

Eventually, I gave in to my feelings and exploded in anger. With my nasty and sinful attitude now exposed, the Spirit's conviction was quick. *You have a heart problem*, God said. *Let's chat about the gentle and quiet spirit this week, shall we?*

Our verses are straightforward: Gentleness and quietness are beautiful. Harshness and loudness are not.

Take it from me. This is a lesson you want to learn on the page, not through experience.

In the Sermon on the Mount, Jesus used the similar word *meek* to describe the gentle and quiet spirit. "Blessed are the meek, for they shall inherit the earth" (Matt. 5:5). Jesus was literally promising the world to the gentle in spirit.

In contrast, just a few chapters later, he scorched the religious leaders for spewing speech that revealed deep hypocrisy. "For out of the abundance of the heart the mouth speaks. . . . I tell you, on the day of judgment people will give account for every careless word they speak" (12:34, 36).

Jesus wasn't kidding around. What comes out of our mouths is serious, eternal business.

When we lash out in anger or are harsh, demanding, critical, or demeaning to our husbands, our children, cashiers—*anyone*—we will give an account for it later.

Good thing there's great news.

What God promised Israel if they sought him in repentance he promises us still today: a fresh start in Christ.

"And I will give you a new heart, and a new spirit I will put within you. And I will remove the hearts of stone from your flesh and give you a heart of flesh" (Ezek. 36:26).

We get a do-over when we repent of sin and turn our hearts over to Jesus. Many do-overs. No matter how hard or harsh our hearts, it's not too late for any of us.

There is always hope in Christ.

1 . When it comes to your words, is there a specific area where you struggle? Harshness? Irritability? Gossip? Ask the Lord to help you identify if there is sin in your heart that might be at the root of this struggle. Could it be fear? Selfishness? Distrust? Envy?

_____

_____

_____

2 . We don't have to tackle wayward speech in our own power. Consider adding this verse to your daily prayers: "Set a guard, O Lord, over my mouth; keep watch over the door of my lips!" (Ps. 141:3).

_____

_____

_____

DAY 4

Do not let your adorning be external—the braiding of hair and the putting on of gold jewelry, or the clothing you wear—but let your adorning be the hidden person of the heart with the imperishable beauty of a gentle and quiet spirit, which in God's sight is very precious.
1 PETER 3:3-4

"How's your heart?"

It's a question Josh and I picked up at a marriage conference a few years ago and still ask each other regularly.

It may sound cheesy, but it's an excellent way to cut through the small talk and get to the deep stuff. *What's really going on in you? Is there anything hidden in your heart that needs to come to light?*

It's a question I had to ask myself after my Vesuvius-level eruption at Josh last week. *What was going on in my heart? Why did submitting make me so angry?*

Peter gives us a tiny clue to the secret of submission in the verse that immediately follows our selected passage above. He says, "For this is how the holy women *who hoped in God* used to adorn themselves" (1 Pet. 3:5, italics mine).

Why were the holy women of old gentle, quiet, and ultimately submissive, according to Peter? Because they were just better people? Because the person they were submitting to always deserved it? Nope.

Because they put their hope in God.

Often, in marriage, we will justify our reluctance to submit because we feel we cannot trust our husbands' leadership. Yet God calls us to let our husbands lead, *not* because they will lead perfectly *but because God will*.

When we submit, we are living out our beliefs that God will do right by us. Our hope is in him alone. He is faithful to lead us well, even if our husbands or bosses or governments are not.

He assures, "I will instruct you and teach you in the way you should go; I will counsel you with my loving eye on you. Do not be like the horse or mule, which have no understanding but must be controlled by bit and bridle or they will not come to you" (Ps. 32:8–9 NIV).

An animal that refuses to be led will be bridled. If we resist submission, we buck against God. The consequences are unpleasant, but the alternative is praiseworthy.

Trust God's heart for you. Trust his leadership of your family. Whether you are married or single, God promises to lead you well. Submit your heart to his perfect care and put your hope in him.

Hoping in God is the secret to submission.

1. How is your heart? David asked God to search and know him and see if there was anything grievous in him (Ps. 139:23–24). We would be wise to do the same. Take time right now to let God reveal anything in your heart that needs to be brought into the light.

_____

_____

_____

_____

2. What are you putting your hope in today?

_____

_____

_____

_____

DAY 5

Do not let your adorning be external—the braiding of hair and the putting on of gold jewelry, or the clothing you wear—but let your adorning be the hidden person of the heart with the imperishable beauty of a gentle and quiet spirit, which in God's sight is very precious.

Here's the rub.

The trouble with the gentle and quiet spirit is that it's so, well . . . gentle and quiet.

By definition, it doesn't demand attention or announce itself loudly. It's often unnoticed and rarely gets praised. It generally doesn't garner a large platform or get the recognition it deserves.

Gentle and quiet can just feel so unseen. And no one wants to feel unseen.

Yet this is one of those faith-deepening places where we must cling to what we *know* is true rather than what may feel true.

The hidden person of our hearts—when she embraces the imperishable, hope-soaked beauty of the gentle and quiet spirit—"in God's sight is very precious." In fact, it seems that when we are unseen, we are actually the most *seen* we will ever be.

Quiet blazes loud and clear in God's view. Gentleness grabs his attention. God's perfect vision sees what the rest of the world doesn't, and he counts it as precious. Costly. Of great worth.

That's right. God's upside-down ways strike again.

Yes, we may still serve in obscurity. We may faithfully submit to someone who never quite appreciates it. We may look foolish for putting our hopes in a God we cannot see. *But he sees us.* He recognizes our obedient hearts and is faithful to reward. "For the eyes of the LORD range throughout the earth to strengthen those whose hearts are fully committed to him" (2 Chron. 16:9 NIV).

Submission may make us feel weak, but God rewards it with strength.

Gentleness and quietness may feel small, but God beholds them as precious.

Hoping in God may feel uncertain, but God promises us himself, the most Certain One there is.

And when we fail to believe it or to remember it or to act on what we know, which we inevitably will, we can fall back, yet again, on God's intimate knowledge of our inner persons. "For whenever our heart condemns us, God is greater than our heart, and he knows everything" (1 John 3:20).

There is no way around it. On our best days and our worst days—at our most beautiful and our most ugly—God sees, knows, and loves us still.

Put your hope in the Lord, beloved. You are beautiful in his sight.

1. How "seen" do you feel today? Does this feeling change with your circumstances? How does the truth of 2 Chronicles 16:9 encourage you when you feel unseen?

_____

_____

_____

2. Spend a few minutes being quiet before the Lord. Let him speak to your heart. What does he say?

_____

_____

_____

DAY 6

Do not let your adorning be external—the braiding of hair and the putting on of gold jewelry, or the clothing you wear—but let your adorning be the hidden person of the heart with the imperishable beauty of a gentle and quiet spirit, which in God's sight is very precious.   1 PETER 3:3–4

Take a few minutes today to journal and reflect on what God revealed to your heart through our verses this week. What did you learn about yourself or God? Is there a sin you need to confess and turn from or a truth you need to apply to your life? How have you been changed by meditating on this passage?

DAY 7

Do not let your adorning be external—the braiding of hair and the putting on of gold jewelry, or the clothing you wear—but let your adorning be the hidden person of the heart with the imperishable beauty of a gentle and quiet spirit, which in God's sight is very precious.

1 PETER 3:3–4

Close your week by praying the Word back to the Lord. Then rest! God's promises are true. Let them satisfy and quiet your heart today.

Holy Spirit, do a work in me. Forgive me when I let my adorning become externally focused. And where I resist submission, soften my heart. Teach me to adorn the hidden person of my heart with gentleness, quietness, and hope. Thank you for seeing me, Father, and for reminding me that I am precious in your sight. Amen.

Week 8

PROVERBS 19:21

DAY 1

Many are the plans in the mind of a man, but it is the purpose of the
LORD that will stand.   PROVERBS 19:21

My husband and I have five kids. Our youngest is three, which means we have survived the terrible twos enough times that you can reasonably take our word for it when we swear by the following: three is worse.

Though they distract you with adorableness, three-year-olds have discovered a dangerous weapon: their own wills. Try to prevent them from wielding the toothpaste, your sewing scissors, or a chainsaw, and warfare is in order. Three-year-olds want to be in charge.

Then again, who doesn't?

Our passage this week meets this very issue head-on. It's found in Proverbs, a book primarily written by King Solomon, who was blessed with extraordinary wisdom straight from God. It was Solomon who advised, "The beginning of wisdom is this: Get wisdom, and whatever you get, get insight" (Prov. 4:7).

To be wise, we must seek wisdom. And we'll need it this week.

The topic we're addressing is not easy—in many ways it's just plain mysterious—but it cannot be avoided if we want to grow in our faith. It's *that* important.

Because just as ridiculously frustrating as it is to try to convince someone who was only recently potty-trained that they, in fact, don't get to call the shots in life, we are hardly different. We may make our plans, and our plans may be good—even God-honoring—but verses like this confront us with the truth.

We absolutely do not get to be in control. God absolutely does.

God's sovereignty—his in-chargeness—is an unavoidable and constant presence throughout his Word. We must face this reality before we go a moment further.

Either God is God, King of Kings and Lord of Lords, seated on an eternal throne, reigning over all of life, or he's not. If he isn't, you can close this book and move on. A not-in-control God offers us no hope.

But if he is—if God is sovereign over both the good and the bad in our lives, if his purposes will always stand, even down to the roll of the dice (Prov. 16:33)—then we have hope.

Though our verse appears short and simple, I believe we'll find within it unexpected riches this week. A bigger God, steadier faith, deeper joy.

Let's let God reign. He already does anyway.

1. Write Proverbs 19:21 on a note card and work on memorizing it this week. Hiding the Word in your heart will prove to be a beneficial and long-lasting companion to your time of meditation.

2. Psalm 115:3 says, "Our God is in the heavens; he does all that he pleases." What are the implications of this verse to the world? What about to your life specifically? Does this comfort you or make you uncomfortable? Why?

DAY 2

Many are the plans in the mind of a man, but it is the purpose of the LORD that will stand.   PROVERBS 19:21

Nine years ago, I made big plans. I would take my first book to a writers' conference. I would pitch it to a particular editor. That editor would love it, and it would sell bajillions.

So I did. But it didn't.

I took that book to the conference. The editor I had planned to pitch it to was a no-show. The next-in-line editor didn't love my book, and it most certainly didn't sell bajillions. (Not even ba-hundreds.)

Fortunately, I would later learn, God's plans were better than mine anyway.

God's sovereignty is clear throughout Scripture. Consider Daniel 4:35: "He does according to his will . . . and none can stay his hand or say to him, 'What have you done?'" Or Job 23:13: "What he desires, that he does."

God is absolutely, fully in charge. What he decrees happens.

Yet Scripture also teaches simultaneously that we are responsible for our part in his plan. We will be held accountable for our actions.

Consider the words of Paul: "For we are his workmanship, created in Christ Jesus for good works, which God prepared beforehand, *that we should walk in them*" (Eph. 2:10, italics mine).

Hear that? Before we were born, God made plans for us.

Our part is to walk in them.

God won't do the walking for us. We are responsible for our steps. Steps going forward or steps going back.

We see it in the betrayal of Jesus carried out by Judas Iscariot. Jesus said, "The Son of Man goes as it is written of him, but woe to that man by whom the Son of Man is betrayed!" (Matt. 26:24).

Though Jesus's betrayal had been decreed from before time, Judas would still face eternal punishment for his role in Jesus's death.

Humans are absolutely, fully responsible for their actions.

God's sovereignty and our responsibility run as parallel truths in the Bible. In our limited understanding, we may never fully grasp how this can be, but we can know this: A good God is in charge, and we have an important role in his plans.

Nine years ago, I worked hard to write the best book I could, then I nervously stepped out in faith and took it to that conference. Though the script of my life had been written from before time, I still had an active part to play in the story.

I made my plans, but God's purposes prevailed. They always do. Praise God! They always do.

1. David said of God, "You are good and do good" (Ps. 119:68). How does this simple truth help us to praise God for his sovereignty?

2. Consider a time when your plans did not work out the way you wanted. What did you learn about God or yourself through that experience that you may not have learned had things gone as you'd expected?

DAY 3

Many are the plans in the mind of a man, but it is the purpose of the
LORD that will stand. PROVERBS 19:21

I dated my husband before he was a believer.

Nope, it wasn't done in ignorance. I knew better. We were unequally yoked. I was not walking in the ways of God, and my refusal to heed biblical instruction on this matter had some difficult consequences.

Yet I've also been married to this same man for sixteen years, and he's now a godly husband and worship pastor. We have five wonderful children. Despite our beginnings, being married to Josh has become one of the greatest blessings of my life.

God had a good plan for me *and, somehow, he used my mistakes to accomplish it.*

It reminds me of the life of Joseph.

Joseph had unintentionally angered his own brothers to the point that they sold him into slavery. For years after, he lived a roller-coaster life of great highs and desperate lows, eventually culminating in his being named to one of the highest positions in Egyptian government. God would use him in that position to prepare the region for a forthcoming devastating famine.

Later, when his brothers unknowingly came to Joseph for help, Joseph revealed his true identity without bitterness. In fact, he used the opportunity to preach God's sovereignty to his brothers then and to us now.

"As for you, you meant evil against me, but God meant it for good, to bring it about that many people should be kept alive, as they are today" (Gen. 50:20).

God used Joseph's difficult life for a good purpose.

Yet what often gets overlooked is that God also used Joseph's brothers' lives for a good purpose.

Despite their grievous sin, they and their families did not starve to death, *because they sold Joseph into slavery.*

This is an almost unfathomable truth. Yet this is the God we serve.

Our God is able to take our less-than-perfect decisions and turn them for our good. He is able to justly punish sin and, at the same time, be "kind to the ungrateful and the evil" (Luke 6:35). He is able to promise, amazingly, "I will be merciful toward their iniquities, and I will remember their sins no more" (Heb. 8:12).

God's in-chargeness is intricately intertwined with his mercy, his kindness.

He is unfailingly faithful, even when we have not been faithful.

My life is proof. God can redeem anything, anyone.

Rest, beloved. God's plans for you are plans of hope.

1. In what specific areas of your life have you seen God redeem your mistakes for his glory? Spend time in prayer thanking him for this mercy today.

2. What sins or mistakes in your past are you still waiting on God to redeem? Read Psalm 103:11–13 as God's own words spoken directly to you, his precious child.

DAY 4

Many are the plans in the mind of a man, but it is the purpose of the
LORD that will stand.   PROVERBS 19:21

Proverbs 19:21 has been a theme in my life over the last few years. There's just no way around it; I've made my plans, but God's purposes have stood.

It's become a life verse for me, reminding me time and again that God's plans for me will stand. Which is not a hard thing to stomach when life is good.

It's when life is not so good that things get a bit dicey.

When God sovereignly allows us to experience troubles, hardship, even tragedy, what in the world do we do with this truth? Is there any comfort in it at all? How do we understand this passage in light of the increasingly difficult reality we are living in?

I've heard it said that the best commentary on Scripture is Scripture. Meaning that when we can't understand something in the Bible, the first place we should turn is back to the Bible. We allow God to illuminate truth first, before anyone else.

Which is why Proverbs 3:5–6 is my other life verse.

> Trust in the LORD with all your heart,
>   and do not lean on your own understanding.
> In all your ways acknowledge him,
>   and he will make straight your paths.

There's a reason this verse is so beloved among believers. There's a reason I write it in every card I send to high school graduates. There's a reason King Solomon included this among his first instructions on wisdom.

Life will throw curveballs. We will not understand God's ways. His purposes will sometimes seem unclear, wrong, even destructive. We cannot lean on our own understanding because our own understanding will fail us.

God will not.

When we trust in the Lord with all our hearts—believing that we were created for good works, which God prepared beforehand—and choose therefore to lean not on our understanding but instead to walk in the plans God has for us, what does the Word say?

He will make our paths straight.

Life may seem dark, the way before us uncertain, but when we walk in the purposes of God, he promises that he will make the path ahead sure and straight.

Which means we can proceed in faith, even when we do not understand. God's sovereignty *is* a good, straight pathway through dark, uncertain places.

Trust him.

1. Why is it so important to turn to God's Word first when we have questions about life? What is the danger in seeking other sources before we seek answers in Scripture?

_____

_____

_____

2. What dark places are you walking through right now? Meditate on our verse alongside Proverbs 3:5–6 and let these complementary truths renew your mind today.

DAY 5

I went to that first writers' conference with plans to get just one
book published.

Instead, I ended up at an unexpected meeting with an unexpected editor that resulted in not just one but eleven books being
published.

God said no to my plans.

Thank goodness.

God's sovereignty is not just a fancy piece of theology; God's sovereignty is a ballast in the storm of life. It's truth we can walk in. Wisely,
confidently, and *fearlessly*.

A. W. Pink lived generations ago, but his words are timeless: "Without
a doubt, a world-crisis is at hand, and everywhere men are alarmed. But
God is not! . . . It is no unexpected emergency that now confronts Him,
for He is the One who 'works all things after the counsel of his own will'
(Eph. 1:11). Hence, though the world is panic-stricken, the word to the
believer is, 'Fear not!' 'All things' are subject to his immediate control."[1]

Nothing we are facing today is out of his hands. Nothing we face
tomorrow will surprise him. Even yesterday's mistakes, through his marvelous mercy, can be transformed into blessings. With God, "all things"
means all things.

But just in case we're still not convinced that God being entirely in
charge of "all things" is good news, Paul echoes this phrase in another
well-loved verse: "And we know that for those who love God *all things*
work together for good, for those who are called according to his purpose"
(Rom. 8:28, italics mine).

When we love the Lord, his purposes are for our good. For a hope and a future. Not only for now but for all eternity. Because of "the unchangeable character of his purpose" (Heb. 6:17), we can rejoice. His good plans for us cannot be altered. "We have this as a sure and steadfast anchor of the soul, a hope that enters into the inner place behind the curtain, where Jesus has gone as a forerunner on our behalf" (vv. 19–20).

Christ has anchored us to a loving and gracious God who "is able to do far more abundantly than all that we ask or think" (Eph. 3:20).

Why, oh why, beloved sister, would we want anything but God's plans for us anyway?

1. "The counsel of the Lord stands forever, the plans of his heart to all generations" (Ps. 33:11). We do not serve a heartless God. How does this precious truth about him comfort your heart today?

_____

_____

_____

2. Are you fearful about the future, or does it seem uncertain? Write your fears down today, and hand them over to the Lord in prayer. Every time they come to mind, cast them back on him. He cares for you.

_____

_____

_____

_____

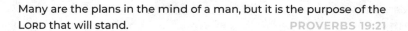

DAY 6

Many are the plans in the mind of a man, but it is the purpose of the LORD that will stand.
PROVERBS 19:21

Take a few minutes today to journal and reflect on what God revealed to your heart through our verse this week. What did you learn about yourself or God? Is there a sin you need to confess and turn from or a truth you need to apply to your life? How have you been changed by meditating on this passage?

DAY 7

Many are the plans in the mind of a man, but it is the purpose of the
LORD that will stand.

*Close your week by praying the Word back to the Lord. Then rest! God's
promises are true. Let them satisfy and quiet your heart today.*

*Lord God, you are in charge. I am not. I have so many
plans I think are best, but it is your purposes that will stand.
Forgive me when I run ahead of you, and teach me to trust
in your perfect sovereignty. Amen.*

Week 9

ROMANS 8:1–2

DAY 1

There is therefore now no condemnation for those who are in Christ
Jesus. For the law of the Spirit of life has set you free in Christ Jesus
from the law of sin and death. ROMANS 8:1-2

During a season of rebellion many years ago, I allowed a grievous
sin to seep into my life. The enemy was crafty; he knew better
than to tempt me with it all at once.

Instead, he wooed me gently with promises of pleasure. He lured me
with little compromises. He whispered and seduced and coaxed just loud
enough to drown out the Holy Spirit's conviction.

No one will know, he said. *It will be worth it,* he said.

And I believed him.

Then, years later, that particular sin struggle long behind me, I realized with astonishment one day that the enemy was *still* after me, and
over that very same thing.

Only this time he shouted.

Look what you did!

Condemnation, I learned, is one of the enemy's favorite games.

Paul wrote Romans 8 while seemingly swept up in adoration and
worship of the Lord. The entire chapter is gloriously good news for the
believer. We would all do well to study and memorize the whole of it.

But let's allow these first two verses to sweep us away for now, as they
are powerful truths against the tireless enemy we all will fight, some of
us hourly.

As believers, when we sin, we can expect to experience the pressing
and gentle conviction of the Holy Spirit as he leads us to repentance and
restoration with our Father.

On the flip side, the enemy, always two-faced, encourages us to sin with promises of happiness, then, if we give in, dive-bombs us with condemnation. *Look what you've done,* he says. *You're ruined.*

Beloved, this is not from the Lord! Condemnation never is.

So we must be prepared. Meditation on and memorization of the Word are two of the most practical and effective weapons in the believer's arsenal. Romans 8:1–2 is not just lofty spiritual talk; it is our slam-dunk case against the enemy's assault.

Store up these verses. Be ready. Recognize the attack and respond with truth. *For you have been set free. Never to return again.*

Praise him! For those who are in Christ, there never has been, never is, and never will be any condemnation from the Lord.

1. Write Romans 8:1–2 on a note card and work on memorizing it this week. Hiding the Word in your heart will prove to be a beneficial and long-lasting companion to your time of meditation.

2. If you have time, read all of Romans 8. Enjoy the gusto with which Paul praises the Lord, and pray that God would give you that kind of enthusiasm and joy in Christ.

DAY 2

There is therefore now no condemnation for those who are in Christ Jesus. For the law of the Spirit of life has set you free in Christ Jesus from the law of sin and death.   ROMANS 8:1–2

I am a seminary dropout.

This needs to be said.

As I pondered writing this devotional, the reality of my unfinished education haunted me. What if the women reading this book find out? Will I lose credibility in their eyes? Will they keep reading?

But it is what it is. There's no changing or denying it. Biblical higher education–wise, I am a failure.

I enrolled in an online seminary shortly after having my first child. Home all day with a baby who napped blessedly well, I had time on my hands. *Seminary it is!* (said the *completely* naïve new mother). It wasn't until the napping baby transitioned into a busy toddler that I realized my error. *I do not have time for this.* And I dropped out.

Though that happened years ago, the enemy has drawn on it fresh, almost daily, since I began this project. *Who are you to write for women? You're not educated. You're not qualified. You are inadequate. Who do you think you are?*

These condemning thoughts have plagued me for months, and it took me a long, long time to stop letting them paralyze me. Because the thing is, they're true.

I *am* a Bible-school dropout. I am *not* qualified. I *am* inadequate. And, to top it all off, I am *sinful.*

We all are. We have fallen short of the glory of God. Even our tiniest sins are worthy of his wrath. And our enemy knows it. Revelation 12:10

says he stands before the throne of God, accusing us day and night. And his charges against us are legit. We deserve death.

Yet we live. We are not found guilty. The case is closed against us, even as our only defense—our only hope for acquittal—depends amazingly, solely on those teensy little words at the end of Romans 8:1, "in Christ Jesus."

We are guilty, but we are counted as righteous in Christ. The blood of the Lamb has silenced our accuser (Rev. 12:11). His accusations against us have been dismissed, nailed to the cross (Col. 2:13–14). And we are set free.

Who do you think you are?

You are in Christ Jesus.

1. Is there a past mistake or current struggle the enemy won't let you forget? Lay it down right now before the cross. Seek forgiveness if it is unconfessed, and claim the promise of this week's passage. You are free.

2. What tasks or calling are you facing for which you feel spiritually inadequate? Read Ephesians 1:16–19. How do these words assure you that you are not underequipped in God?

DAY 3

There is therefore now no condemnation for those who are in Christ Jesus. For the law of the Spirit of life has set you free in Christ Jesus from the law of sin and death. ROMANS 8:1-2

I recently watched the movie *Harriet*, a 2019 biopic about Harriet Tubman, the fugitive slave turned courageous conductor on the Underground Railroad.

In a powerful scene near the end of the film, Harriet beseeches her fellow abolitionists not to give up on their mission, even though the task is becoming increasingly difficult. She reminds her audience of the horrors of slavery, which many, like her, had experienced firsthand, and she rebukes them for their hesitation to continue rescuing slaves. She scolds, "You've been free so long you forgot what it's like."

Our verses this week speak of two laws, one of which governs every soul walking on this earth. Each of us is either a slave to the law of sin and death or free under the law of the Spirit of life. There is no third law. No middle ground. It's one or the other.

Before salvation in Christ, this law of sin and death most certainly governed us all. The truth about our former state is woven heavily throughout Paul's writings: We were dead in the trespasses and sins in which we once walked (Eph. 2:1–2). We were slaves to sin (Rom. 6:17), trapped by our fleshly desires (Eph. 2:3), unable to do what was right (Rom. 3:10), and subject to God's righteous wrath because of it (6:23).

As believers, however, we are mercifully no longer under that bondage. Praise God, this law that leads to death does not apply to us now. But here's where we go wrong. Many of us have been free so long we've forgotten what our former bondage was like.

But we must not.

When we forget the horrors of what we've been rescued from, we can end up inadvertently ignoring the plights of others who are still enslaved. People we love, our unbelieving family, friends, children, coworkers. This law of sin and death is their current reality. They are enslaved and unable to save themselves.

But we have the rescue plan, don't we? The gospel!

And how could we, remembering where we've come from, keep it to ourselves?

Seeking to release slaves is never easy, but it is a cause always worth fighting for.

Let's join God in setting captives free *today*.

1. Sharing the gospel can be extremely intimidating. How does regularly reflecting on our own former spiritual slavery cause us to appreciate the grace we've been shown and motivate us to share this good news with others?

2. Whose salvation are you praying for? Make a list. As often as they come to mind, ask God to rescue them from their bondage.

DAY 4

> There is therefore now no condemnation for those who are in Christ Jesus. For the law of the Spirit of life has set you free in Christ Jesus from the law of sin and death. ROMANS 8:1-2

I'm a bit of a word snob. Meaningless expressions drive me bonkers.

A recent ad campaign for a casino in my area induced many an eye roll out of me. Plastered on billboards overlooking the interstate, attractive men and busty women rolled dice, hit jackpots, and laughed (seemingly) nonstop. Splashed across their antics were the words "Live like you mean it."

Now, I've been in a casino a time or two, and whatever "Live like you mean it" is supposed to describe is not at all what I saw there. Blank expressions; thick air; jangly, mechanical noises: this is not living.

Or at least, this is not what living is meant to be.

We spoke of bad news yesterday, the law of sin and death. Today, we'll focus on the good news. Namely, for believers, that the law of the Spirit of life has set us free in Christ Jesus.

This Spirit of life is the Holy Spirit, whom God sends to dwell with believers from the first moment of their salvation.

The Spirit's presence within us not only assures that we are sealed in Christ for all eternity but also holds powerful promises for us here and now. Paul tells us, "For to set the mind on the flesh is death, but to set the mind on the Spirit is life and peace" (Rom. 8:6).

Life and peace.

Isn't that what everyone wants? Like the casino ad and a million ads before and after it, isn't that the great promise? Come *here* to live. Buy *this* to have peace.

But the Word tells us that life and peace are found in only one place. *And, if we have trusted in Christ, he lives within us.*

Near the time of his death, Jesus assured his followers that it was to their advantage that he was going away, for they would not be left alone (John 16:7). God would send the Helper, the Holy Spirit, in his place. Jesus promised, "Peace I leave with you; my peace I give to you" (John 14:27). Though they would not have Jesus in the flesh much longer, they would have his life-giving Spirit *and* they would have his peace.

And still now we have this promise, beloved. True life. True peace. Which cannot nor ever will be found in any place apart from Christ.

1. It's tempting to look for life and peace through money, quiet getaways, shopping, etc. In what areas are you personally vulnerable to associating life and peace with something other than Christ?

2. How does reflecting on the promise that the Spirit of life lives inside you set you free today?

DAY 5

There is therefore now no condemnation for those who are in Christ Jesus. For the law of the Spirit of life has set you free in Christ Jesus from the law of sin and death.   ROMANS 8:1–2

Just before we had our third baby, we decided it was time to upgrade the station wagon to a minivan. Once we found the one we wanted, I was shocked. I had no idea what I'd been missing. Those automatic sliding doors delighted my exhausted little heart.

One morning, after buckling in the kids, I said out loud, "Thank you, Jesus, for this van." From the back, the voice of my preschool-age daughter chimed loudly, "'You're welcome,' Jesus said."

If you were able to take the time to read through all of Romans 8 this week, you may have noticed how different these verses are from much of Paul's other writings. He often laced his letters with commandments or rules for holy living, like those we studied in 1 Thessalonians in week 3.

But there are no commandments in Romans 8. Not a single imperative for the reader to follow. Rather, Paul spends this entire chapter reflecting on all we've received in Christ: life in the Spirit, freedom from sin and death, love that overflows with redemption and peace.

The chapter even closes with surely one of the most powerful rhetorical questions ever written: "If God is for us, who can be against us?" (v. 31).

Paul's delight and confidence in Christ seem unflappable, but we must remember that Paul was still just a human, with his own past failures and present struggles. There is little doubt he was just as susceptible to condemnation during his life as we are.

The enemy would have had plenty of ammunition to aim his way too. *Weren't you the one who persecuted the followers of Christ? Who are you to try to become one of them? Who are you to teach them? Who are you . . . ?*

Thankfully, Paul fought back and gave us Romans 8:1–2 to lob at our relentless accuser. These verses are a mantra for the believer. They should be hidden in our hearts and ready on our lips.

Who am I?

I am not condemned.

I am in Christ Jesus.

I am free.

I am alive.

I am the one whom God is for.

Thank you, Jesus.

("You're welcome," Jesus said.)

---

1. Put this passage into practice. Anytime condemnation or shame attacks today, immediately hand it over to the Lord in prayer and remind yourself of who you are in Christ. You'll be shocked by how quickly Christ will set you free.

2. How have you done at memorizing our verses this week? Keep at it! These verses are too powerful to not have them hidden in your heart.

DAY 6

There is therefore now no condemnation for those who are in Christ Jesus. For the law of the Spirit of life has set you free in Christ Jesus from the law of sin and death. ROMANS 8:1–2

Take a few minutes today to journal and reflect on what God revealed to your heart through our verses this week. What did you learn about yourself or God? Is there a sin you need to confess and turn from or a truth you need to apply to your life? How have you been changed by meditating on this passage?

DAY 7

There is therefore now no condemnation for those who are in Christ Jesus. For the law of the Spirit of life has set you free in Christ Jesus from the law of sin and death.   ROMANS 8:1–2

Close your week by praying the Word back to the Lord. Then rest! God's promises are true. Let them satisfy and quiet your heart today.

Praise you, Jesus! *Because of my sin, I deserve death. Yet I am not condemned. The Spirit of life has set me free in you. I am no longer a slave to sin and death. Help me not to forget this gift, and give me boldness to share it with others. Amen.*

Week 10

NEHEMIAH 8:10

DAY 1

Eighth grade was a real low point for me.

On the first day of school, I found myself deeply intimidated by the no-nonsense football coach teaching my math class that year. While assigning textbooks, he called each of us to his desk individually to write our name in our book. On my turn, I bent down to sign but found I couldn't.

For a brief and terrible moment, I forgot my name.

My own name.

Even for an insecure fourteen-year-old, that's one thing I really ought to have been sure of.

I wasn't too sure about our verse for this week either, honestly. It just seems so . . . lightweight. *Is there enough to learn through this verse to merit spending seven days on it?* It's only nine words long, after all.

But as I began to study, I noticed something.

God's name, "the LORD," is tucked right in the middle of those nine words. Anytime we see "the LORD" in all caps in Scripture, we're seeing the English translation of the Hebrew proper name for God, *yhwh*, which we pronounce "Yahweh."

I was surprised to learn that because the original Hebrew manuscripts primarily used consonants in their spelling, the *a* and *e* in Yahweh were added in later by scholars to help us pronounce this otherwise difficult, vowelless word.

Therefore, the way we say God's name is based, at least somewhat, on a scholarly guess.

I was shocked.

For all we think we know about God and his Word, we aren't even sure we have his name right.

This little insight alone silenced my concerns. Who am I to think that we have tapped out the resources of God's eternal words? There is more truth to be found in Scripture than we can ever seek out. There are treasures inside beyond what we'll ever know.

So we'll treasure-hunt this week.

Together we'll dig in, and we'll find in our verse the promise of joy, overflowing with the blessing of strength.

Nine words that will remind us who God is, what he has done, and what he is *still* doing.

We will be strengthened with joy, and, I pray, we will cry out together, "Oh, the depth of the riches and wisdom and knowledge of God!" (Rom. 11:33).

1. Write Nehemiah 8:10 on a note card and work on memorizing it this week. Hiding the Word in your heart will prove to be a beneficial and long-lasting companion to your time of meditation.

2. Read the one-verse parable in Matthew 13:44: "The kingdom of heaven is like treasure hidden in a field, which a man found and covered up. Then in his joy he goes and sells all that he has and buys that field." Do you feel this same kind of excitement as you seek God in his Word? Why or why not?

_____

_____

_____

_____

_____

DAY 2

Our little verse this week is very often quoted. (I can even sing you a *super* annoying song based on it from my childhood. But I won't.) Yet it's found in a not-very-often-read Old Testament book.

Nehemiah tells the story of God's people returning to their homeland of Jerusalem after years in exile in Babylon, sometime around 430 BC.

Nehemiah—a Jewish cupbearer to a pagan king—was granted permission to return and rebuild Jerusalem's walls, which had been torn down and burned. Nehemiah faced much opposition but managed to complete the massive undertaking in fifty-two days.

The newly returned Jews gathered together and requested that the Book of the Law be read. But what most likely began as a day of celebration quickly turned to mourning.

Whether they had forgotten God's commandments over the years or simply ignored them, on this day, they heard the Law and realized how far they had strayed.

And they wept.

And God heard.

Nehemiah was God's mouthpiece of grace over his people. Go and celebrate this holy day, God said. "And do not be grieved, for the joy of the LORD is your strength."

What we have here is the most delightfully beautiful reminder that we serve a kindhearted God, a God who deeply desires our restoration.

When we consider our sin, past and current, grief is the appropriate response, and repentance is the right next step. And not so God can say "I told you so," but so he can say "I love you so."

In place of godly grief, God offers joy.

"I will give thanks to you, O LORD, for though you were angry with me, your anger turned away, that you might comfort me. . . . With joy you will draw water from the wells of salvation" (Isa. 12:1, 3).

The wells of God's salvation are bottomless. *Years* of rebellion on Israel's part couldn't plumb their depths. No sin we've committed or will ever commit can either. With joy, we're welcome to come and drink deeply and often of his unending grace.

However badly you messed up yesterday or will mess up today, beloved, do not be grieved over your sin a moment longer.

Repent and celebrate, for repentance yields joy.

1. Take a moment to thank God that the well of his forgiveness never runs dry. This is easy to take for granted, yet it is one of the most profound ways in which our God is set apart from the gods of every other world religion.

2. Read Isaiah 12:1–3. How do these verses combat the dangerous worldviews that God is either unconcerned with sin or condemning and unforgiving when we do sin?

_____

_____

_____

_____

_____

DAY 3

For the joy of the LORD is your strength.

NEHEMIAH 8:10

While Nehemiah and his fellow Jews labored to rebuild Jerusalem's walls, the equivalent of the neighborhood bullies wandered over to pester and jeer. "Yes, what they are building," they said, "if a fox goes up on it he will break down their stone wall!" (Neh. 4:3).

(These guys could have used a few lessons in throwing insults. My preschool-age boys can do better than that.)

But then their childish taunts turned vicious, and they began plotting to kill those working on the wall. Nehemiah caught wind and encouraged his fellow workers not to back down. "Do not be afraid of them. Remember the Lord, who is great and awesome" (v. 14).

Remember the Lord.

There is surely no better advice one can offer.

Recharged in their mission, each builder "labored on the work with one hand and held his weapon with the other" (v. 17).

They remembered their Lord, and they were ready to fight for what they had in him.

Remembering what God has done in our lives—his faithfulness to us, the goodness he has poured out, his mercy in grace toward us through Christ Jesus—*this is our ultimate weapon in the fight for joy.*

Our enemy *will* come taunting, but we don't have to sit back and listen.

We stand our ground, weapon in hand, and we do not let go of what we know to be true.

We remember the Lord.

Sometimes (often) the battle we fight will be against ourselves, our own flesh. We find that we are our own bullies. We mourn that we have fallen prey (once again) to our sinful selves. We groan and wonder with Paul, "Wretched man that I am! Who will deliver me from this body of death?" (Rom. 7:24).

And this is our moment.

Either we attack ourselves with insults, or, as Paul did, we choose to remember God and immediately answer our own question with joy: "Thanks be to God through Jesus Christ our Lord!" (v. 25).

Remember the Lord. Remember what God has done for you through Christ. Let God turn your mourning into dancing.

No matter which enemy you face, in Christ alone you will find strength.

1. How is the enemy trying to attack you today? With fear? Discouragement? Anxiety about the future? Write down a promise from the Word that helps you to remember the Lord's faithfulness to you. Need help? Try 2 Thessalonians 3:3.

_____

_____

_____

_____

2. Read how Paul wrestled against his own flesh in Romans 7:15–25. How does this encourage you today?

_____

_____

_____

DAY 4

For the joy of the LORD is your strength.

NEHEMIAH 8:10

We live near a Civil War battlefield. Our house dates back to the mid-1800s. Our driveway was once a section of a nineteenth-century mail route . . . but you wouldn't know it from the junk we find metal-detecting.

Rusty beer cans, pennies from the early 2000s, and gobs of Matchbox cars.

Despite how eager we are for tangible evidence of our property's rich history, the "treasures" we find are, sadly, not much of a testimonial.

The book of Nehemiah, however, is.

God's faithfulness is a theme throughout and a strong testimony to his unchanging character, despite Israel's rebellion against him.

At the dedication of their rebuilt wall, the people renewed their vows to walk in the ways of the Lord. "And they offered great sacrifices that day and rejoiced, for God had made them rejoice with great joy. . . . And the joy of Jerusalem was heard far away" (Neh. 12:43).

Jerusalem's joy was so great it became known to the nations around them. Pagan nations opposed to the Jews and their God must have caught wind of this rejoicing and surely wondered what they were missing.

The Jews' joy in God was a testimony that strengthened them as a nation in the eyes of their enemies.

Their joy in the Lord was their strength.

So it is with us.

No matter how long we have been in the family of faith, we each have our own rich history with God, our personal testimonial of God's faithfulness to us. Our joy in the Lord is a critical part of that testimony.

Unbelievers are watching, and nothing—*nothing*—in us will make them wonder so much at what we have than our joy in the Lord. When they ask our source, we can answer with confidence, "I know whom I have believed" (2 Tim. 1:12).

This joyful testimony in God strengthens us now and until the end. Revelation 12:11 tells us that it will be Christ's sacrificial blood paired with the believers' testimony that finally conquers the enemy.

Our joy in God is meant to strengthen us not only for our sakes but also for those watching and wondering at what they're missing.

Yes, our joy in the Lord is both our greatest strength *and* our greatest influence.

1. Read Nehemiah 9. Notice and underline how often the passage refers to God's mercies, his faithfulness, or the promises he kept to his people.

2. Think over the last week or month. How has God been faithful to you? Is there anyone in your life, believer or unbeliever, with whom you can share this today?

DAY 5

For the joy of the LORD is your strength.

NEHEMIAH 8:10

A few years ago, I gave a talk before a women's group. I had titled it "Becoming a Woman Who Laughs" and based it on Proverbs 31:25, that verse about the God-fearing and joyful woman who laughs at the days to come.

Just before I took the stage, a woman commented to me that she was looking forward to my talk because she loved to laugh. I realized with dread that she and likely others in the crowd were going to come away very disappointed.

My talk was all about suffering.

Joyfulness and suffering may sound like an unlikely pairing, but, in fact, in Scripture they are something of a dynamic duo. The two seem to be, by design, spiritually intertwined.

James tells us to count it all joy when we face trials (James 1:2), and Paul promises that we can "rejoice in our sufferings, knowing that suffering produces endurance, and endurance produces character, and character produces hope" (Rom. 5:3–4).

Paul, perhaps anticipating that we may find hope as the payoff for suffering a smidge disappointing, assures us that it's not. "Hope does not put us to shame, because God's love has been poured into our hearts" (v. 5).

In other words, we will not be disappointed in God's loving answer to our suffering.

Nothing draws us closer to Christ more quickly than pain and trial.

It's in that clinging, desperate, "I need you, Jesus, more than anything else" nearness to him that we will find what seems the most unlikely of rewards. "In your presence there is fullness of joy; at your right hand are pleasures forevermore" (Ps. 16:11).

God's presence is where we find joy. Hope. Strength.

God does not default on his Word. The joy of the Lord is our strength because *it's true*.

God pours his love into our hearts so that we never have to despair. He does not leave us to suffer without the promise of hope and joy to strengthen us.

Be strong in the Lord, dear sister. Remember who he is, what he has done, and what he is *still* doing.

The joy of the Lord is your strength, especially in suffering.

So draw near to him. He will not disappoint.

Joy is coming.

1. Think of a time when you experienced great suffering. How did you experience God strengthening you through joy? If you are suffering now, how is God strengthening you as you draw near to him?

_____

_____

_____

2. Read Hebrews 12:2. Notice that even Jesus pursued joy, suffered to get it, and experienced the reward. Christ can relate to us even in this. How does this encourage you today?

_____

_____

_____

DAY 6

For the joy of the LORD is your strength.
NEHEMIAH 8:10

Take a few minutes today to journal and reflect on what God revealed to your heart through our verse this week. What did you learn about yourself or God? Is there a sin you need to confess and turn from or a truth you need to apply to your life? How have you been changed by meditating on this passage?

DAY 7

For the joy of the LORD is your strength.
NEHEMIAH 8:10

Close your week by praying the Word back to the Lord. Then rest! God's promises are true. Let them satisfy and quiet your heart today.

Heavenly Father, please bring to mind any sin I need to confess, and replace my grief with joy. You are good, merciful, and faithful. Remind me of your love when the enemy comes taunting. Strengthen me, Lord, with your joy, and let my joy point others to you as well. Amen.

Week 11

COLOSSIANS 3:1–3

DAY 1

If then you have been raised with Christ, seek the things that are above, where Christ is, seated at the right hand of God. Set your minds on things that are above, not on things that are on earth. For you have died, and your life is hidden with Christ in God.

COLOSSIANS 3:1–3

Years ago, I heard a news story about an epidemic that was ravaging a third-world country. During the report, an official from the World Health Organization made a profound and memorable statement. "Nothing," she said, "is as contagious as fear."

It's true. Fear, and fear of death in particular, can spread faster and farther than any disease ever could. And, unlike a virus, this fear can infect people for a lifetime.

I know; I've struggled with it. Perhaps you have too. We're certainly not the first.

Fear of death is an ancient problem.

Colossians is a letter penned by Paul to the believers at Colossae. Scholars believe that it was written, at least in part, to address dangerous teachings that had infiltrated the church (see Col. 2:8). They speculate that the Christians at Colossae may have been encouraged to seek means of protection apart from God, perhaps by employing folk traditions like wearing stone amulets inscribed with the names of angels and calling on them to guard the wearer.

What could an amulet do to protect the lives of these believers? Nothing, of course. Yet instead of relying on the Lord to number their days, the Colossians, it seems, may have been grasping at desperate and foolish means of preserving their own lives.

Fear of death took people captive then just as it takes people captive now.

Yet, ironically, the wonderful truths Paul reveals in our passage this week hinge upon the realization that this thing we dread so much—death—is actually the key to life in Christ.

We begin dead in our trespasses (Col. 2:13). Upon receiving Christ, we are "buried with him in baptism" and then "raised with him through faith." (v. 12). With our record of debt now canceled and nailed to the cross (v. 14), God makes us "alive together with him" (v. 13).

The believer's death, burial, and resurrection in Christ is our killing shot in the fight against fear. It's already done. We've already died. We've been raised to life, and our lives are now hidden with Christ. And when physical death does finally come, we have only more life to look forward to.

Beloved, we can rejoice.

Christ has already won over death.

Let's set our hearts and minds on him and not let fear hold us captive a moment longer.

1 · Write Colossians 3:1–3 on a note card and work on memorizing it this week. Hiding the Word in your heart will prove to be a beneficial and long-lasting companion to your time of meditation.

2 · Hebrews 2:15 says that Christ died to "deliver all those who through fear of death were subject to lifelong slavery." How does it change your perspective on the fear of death when you think of it as a form of "lifelong slavery"?

DAY 2

If then you have been raised with Christ, seek the things that are above, where Christ is, seated at the right hand of God. Set your minds on things that are above, not on things that are on earth. For you have died, and your life is hidden with Christ in God.

COLOSSIANS 3:1–3

I recently finished reading the autobiography of Joni Eareckson Tada, a woman who became a quadriplegic after a tragic diving accident in her teens.[1]

Joni recounts the anger, depression, and suicidal thoughts she experienced after realizing her condition was permanent. But God was faithful, and through the death of the use of her limbs, Joni found life.

As we discussed yesterday, our passage this week begins with the foregone conclusion that as believers we have already been crucified with Christ. Therefore, Paul says, since we have also been raised with him, we should "seek the things that are above" (Col. 3:1). The NIV Bible translates this a bit differently: "Set your hearts on things above."

Paul is appealing to us to base our values—the things we love—on God's kingdom. This passage could just as easily be translated "delight in things above" or "desire things above."

This is quite contrary to the way the Christian life is often portrayed: a gloomy, rule-following existence and certainly not something worth delighting in.

Yet Jesus promised that seeking God's kingdom first is the recipe for having everything we need (Matt. 6:33) and, alternately, worth selling everything we have to obtain (13:45–46). David boasted that "those who seek the Lord lack no good thing" (Ps. 34:10).

Oh, how I love these promises.

There are days when I struggle to keep my heart set on things above. I doubt God's goodness. I wonder if he'll provide and if his eternal provisions will be able to satisfy me more than the things of this world.

Yet testimonies like King David's and Joni's remind me that nothing on this earth can compete with the riches we will discover when we set our hearts on God and his kingdom.

Joni said of her experience, "I really began to see suffering in a new light—not as trials to avoid, but as opportunities to 'grab,' because God gives so much of His love, grace, and goodness to those who do."[2]

In times of suffering and of plenty, we are welcome—even *entitled*—as God's children to seek God and *grab* at his goodness.

And it is a promise: When we do, we will not—we *cannot*—be disappointed.

1. Read Matthew 6:19–24, taking special note of verse 21. Take a few moments to evaluate your own heart. What do you treasure?

2. How do you feel about suffering as an opportunity to "grab" at God's goodness toward us? What could this look like in your life, practically speaking? How can you "grab" at God as you suffer?

DAY 3

If then you have been raised with Christ, seek the things that are above, where Christ is, seated at the right hand of God. Set your minds on things that are above, not on things that are on earth. For you have died, and your life is hidden with Christ in God.

COLOSSIANS 3:1–3

I've mentioned I have five kids. I've mentioned they eat three times a day. If you do a little quick math, that means that every day, on average, my husband and I hear 237 arguments about who's supposed to sit where at the dinner table.

A question I will ask God when I get to heaven: "Why, oh why, do kids care so much about where they sit?"

His answer (I assume): "This is why I created seating charts."

It's true. God started it.

Our passage this week makes a point of noting that we should seek the things above, "where Christ is, seated at the right hand of God" (Col. 3:1). Verse after verse in the Bible corroborates this point: Jesus always sits at God's right hand. Why?

Well, because position matters.

Jesus's seat next to his Father signifies his own deity, which he proved to the Pharisees by quoting a psalm about himself: "The Lord said to my Lord, 'Sit at my right hand, until I put your enemies under your feet'" (Matt. 22:44).

It signifies his power. Near the time of his death, the high priest asked Jesus if he was the Christ. "And Jesus said, 'I am, and you will see the Son of Man seated at the right hand of Power, and coming with the clouds of heaven'" (Mark 14:62).

It signifies his intercession to God on our behalf. "We have such a high priest, one who is seated at the right hand of the throne of the Majesty in heaven" (Heb. 8:1).

It signifies his protection. King David said, "Wondrously show your steadfast love, O Savior of those who seek refuge from their adversaries at your right hand" (Ps. 17:7).

And, perhaps my favorite, it declares our own position in relation to Christ. "You make known to me the path of life; in your presence there is fullness of joy; at your right hand are pleasures forevermore" (Ps. 16:11).

Our hopes are not hinged upon a weak, boring, or uninterested god. We delight instead in a deity of power, prayer, protection, and pleasure.

It's no wonder we are to desire things above. Anything else would disappoint.

No one is in a position to care for us like Christ.

1 · Make a list of things in your life that you're worried about right now. How can remembering the significance of Jesus's position at God's right hand change your perspective on those specific concerns?

_____

_____

_____

_____

_____

2 · Hand these concerns over to the Lord in prayer and then cross them off your list. (Really! Do it now.) These worries are no longer a burden that you have to carry.

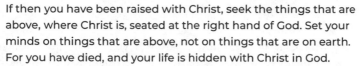

DAY 4

If then you have been raised with Christ, seek the things that are above, where Christ is, seated at the right hand of God. Set your minds on things that are above, not on things that are on earth. For you have died, and your life is hidden with Christ in God.

COLOSSIANS 3:1-3

A dear friend told me about how she recently found herself suddenly overwhelmed by fear and anxiety.

When she sat down to lunch with her seven-year-old son, she decided not to hide that she was struggling. "I'm having a hard day," she told him. "But I know these feelings aren't from the Lord."

Her son, no doubt remembering something she had taught him, responded, "That's right, Mom. Because God is our rock."

A five-minute conversation later, my friend told me, she felt completely at peace, her mind freed from fear. *Because her second grader reminded her to set her mind on things of God.*

I love the practicality and simplicity of this advice.

When we set our minds on things above and not on things on earth, we eliminate the enemy's ability to hijack our hearts. We cannot dwell on sin and Christ at the same time. We cannot get lost in anxiousness if our minds are occupied with the Rock of Ages.

Our minds may be a battlefield, but we've got the weapons to win.

Philippians 4:8 is one of my favorite tools when the enemy attacks: "Finally, brothers, whatever is true, whatever is honorable, whatever is just, whatever is pure, whatever is lovely, whatever is commendable, if there is any excellence, if there is anything worthy of praise, think about these things."

I tend to fear the future. My mind can concoct all kinds of scenarios to worry over.

But when anxiety begins to crowd in, Philippians 4:8 is the test I run my thoughts through. "Finally, brothers, whatever is true . . ." *Is what I'm thinking about true?* I ask myself. *Is it 100 percent definitely going to happen the way I'm imagining it?*

Guess what? I have *never* been able to answer yes to that question. Therefore, if my thoughts are not true, my job is to set my mind on something else, something that *is* true. Something *above*.

It's why having Scripture hidden in our hearts is so important. When our minds are under attack, our hearts must be ready to respond with truth.

Take it from a seven-year-old. God is our rock.

We have a firm place to stand and fight.

1. Do you struggle with anxiety, worry, or fearfulness? What verse can you memorize so that you're ready to fight against those feelings when they attack? (Need some suggestions? Try Joshua 1:9, Matthew 6:25–34, Romans 8:38–39, or Philippians 4:7.)

_____

_____

2. Read 2 Corinthians 10:4–5. Our thought life is a prime location for spiritual warfare. How does it encourage you to "take every thought captive" when the "weapons of our warfare are not of the flesh"?

_____

_____

_____

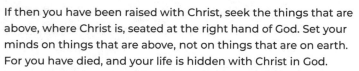

DAY 5

> If then you have been raised with Christ, seek the things that are above, where Christ is, seated at the right hand of God. Set your minds on things that are above, not on things that are on earth. For you have died, and your life is hidden with Christ in God.
>
> COLOSSIANS 3:1–3

Right now, I can think of at least three popular Christian leaders who were recently publicly exposed for moral failures of some kind.

These stories make me sad, and I can't help but wonder if the constant "seen-ness" of their celebrity made them susceptible to dangers most of us will never have to face.

When the latest news broke, I was reminded of my own desire for popularity. I began to realize that the woeful tales of these fallen people could just as easily be mine. It came to mind that I had even recently (sinfully) complained that God had hidden me from the success I desired. I now saw with clarity what an incredible mercy that hiddenness was.

Sister, we are never unseen by God. *But we are hidden.* And that is a very good thing.

We began this week by stating the obvious. Why fear death when we've already been resurrected?

We'll close our week with Paul reminding us (again!) that we've already died and our lives are now hidden with Christ in God.

Perhaps Paul repeated himself because he knew he was speaking to a gal like me, a gal weak in a million ways. Falling back into fears God has already defeated, lusting after success, and pretending I'm strong enough to resist its dangers. Forgetting that though our world is all about being seen, when our lives are hidden with Christ, we are in the best place we can be.

Proverbs 18:10 tells us, "The name of the LORD is a strong tower; the righteous man runs into it and is safe."

The man is afraid. He knows he's weak and can't win. He hightails it to the Lord and hides himself there. *And he is considered righteous because of it.*

David, the famously brave warrior and king, prayed, "Keep me as the apple of your eye; hide me in the shadow of your wings" (Ps. 17:8).

None of us are exempt from needing God's care. All of us would be foolish to draw away from his side.

Whether God gives us wild success or tucks us out of sight, whether we are courageous in him or scramble close to him in fear, we are held and hidden with Christ.

The sweetest and safest place we can be.

1. In your current season of life, do you struggle with feeling unseen, unnoticed, or unappreciated? What do you think God may be teaching you through this time of "hiddenness"?

_____

_____

_____

2. Are there fears that you need to run to the Lord about today? Courage is commendable, but so is humility when it leads us to hide ourselves in the Lord. Give your fears to him today.

_____

_____

_____

DAY 6

If then you have been raised with Christ, seek the things that are above, where Christ is, seated at the right hand of God. Set your minds on things that are above, not on things that are on earth. For you have died, and your life is hidden with Christ in God.

COLOSSIANS 3:1–3

Take a few minutes today to journal and reflect on what God revealed to your heart through our verses this week. What did you learn about yourself or God? Is there a sin you need to confess and turn from or a truth you need to apply to your life? How have you been changed by meditating on this passage?

DAY 7

If then you have been raised with Christ, seek the things that are above, where Christ is, seated at the right hand of God. Set your minds on things that are above, not on things that are on earth. For you have died, and your life is hidden with Christ in God.

COLOSSIANS 3:1–3

Close your week by praying the Word back to the Lord. Then rest! God's promises are true. Let them satisfy and quiet your heart today.

Jesus, thank you for raising me from the dead. Please empower me to seek things above, where you are firmly seated, interceding, protecting, and delighting in me. Keep my mind fixed fully on you, not on earthly things. Thank you that I need not fear death. Thank you that my life is hidden in your hands. Amen.

Week 12

ROMANS 15:13

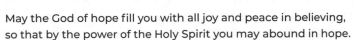

DAY 1

May the God of hope fill you with all joy and peace in believing,
so that by the power of the Holy Spirit you may abound in hope.

ROMANS 15:13

My testimony (the CliffsNotes version):

Good, rule-following little girl grows up in church, walks the aisle to accept Christ, continues being good until she doesn't. Repents. Falls hard for Jesus as a young adult and finally attempts to actually walk with him daily. (Should have done this much sooner.)

My husband's testimony:

Rambunctious little boy doesn't keep rules, rarely goes to church, definitely doesn't try to be good. Makes all the mistakes that rebellious people make before accepting Christ as a young man. Never the same again.

Moral of the story: We are oddly matched.

It's a darn good thing we have Christ in common.

Paul wrote our precious verse this week as a prayer-wish for the believers in the Roman church. Christ-following Jews and gentiles had gathered as one new body with entirely different spiritual backgrounds. There must have been conflict—there always is when blending the rule followers with the rule breakers—but Paul's prayer, for all of them, was the same.

He prayed they would *abound in hope*.

Isn't this a beautiful thought?

Sometimes, for those of us in the grew-up-in-church camp, we've heard the truths of God's Word so often that we've become immune to their potency. We've forgotten (or never understood) the hope that we've received through Christ. In fact, our rule-following has brought us so little joy that we've just about given up on the whole thing.

Why get our hopes up, right?

But our level of spiritual well-being is directly connected to the vibrancy of our hope. Proverbs 13:12 says, "Hope deferred makes the heart sick." Without hope, our hearts cannot thrive. Without something to cling to, we will drop like flies, spiritually speaking.

On the other hand, "a desire fulfilled is a tree of life" (v. 12). Hopes realized can bring a fruitful flourishing in our lives, even as the world around us seems to shrivel.

The hope we have in Christ is the real deal. It promises God's goodness to us now and for eternity. It showcases his mercy, his provision, and his perfect plans for our lives that cannot fail.

Yes, beloved, you have "Christ in you, the hope of glory" (Col. 1:27).

You have every reason to absolutely, completely get your hopes up in him.

---

1. Write Romans 15:13 on a note card and work on memorizing it this week. Hiding the Word in your heart will prove to be a beneficial and long-lasting companion to your time of meditation.

2. How heavily did faith or religion play a role in your upbringing? How has that affected your current understanding or appreciation of the hope you have in Christ?

_____

_____

_____

_____

_____

_____

DAY 2

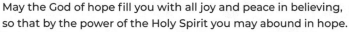

May the God of hope fill you with all joy and peace in believing,
so that by the power of the Holy Spirit you may abound in hope.

ROMANS 15:13

I was helping one of my kids with their homework. The topic was the Greek gods.

Boy, those gods were a bunch of screwups. Reading about them made my heart sad. The ancient Greeks surely found little comfort in worshiping such petty, selfish, fickle gods. Those poor people must have felt so hopeless.

But it was also a teachable moment in our household, as the difference between those man-made gods and our God was so beautifully apparent.

Their gods were gods of heartlessness; ours is the God of hope.

Sit with that for a moment: *the God of hope.*

This is the God who loves us. Even when we don't deserve it.

Take Hosea. Hosea is the true story of God commanding the prophet to take a prostitute as a wife. Her unfaithfulness to Hosea would provide a picture of Israel's faithlessness toward God. But just as Hosea continued to pursue and love his wayward wife, so God promised not only that he would never stop loving his people but also that he would bless them.

Listen to God's tender words: "Therefore, behold, I will allure her, and bring her into the wilderness, and speak tenderly to her. And there I will give her vineyards and make the Valley of Achor a door of hope" (Hosea 2:14–15).

Achor means "trouble."

Our God faithfully pursues his people and turns their trouble into hope.

Despite the many generations between us and the Israelites, God's love for us, his people—rebellious as we are—has not diminished. It has not changed.

This is the God we worship.

Not a god of disappointment. Not a god of harshness. Not a god who longs to run (and ruin) our lives.

He is a good God. A God who joined us here in the flesh. A God who doesn't give up on us, even when we frequently give up on him.

He, the perfect, holy, loving Father.

We, the bunch of screwups. (Yes, us too.)

Let the truth of who God is thrill your heart today.

The God of hope loves you deeply and completely.

Praise God. This is the God you serve.

1. Our modern society may no longer believe in many gods, but it still thinks wrongly about our One True God. Read Jeremiah 9:23–24. How does who God says he is contrast with who the world says he is?

2. Jesus was called Immanuel, meaning "God is with us." Consider how God must feel about you personally to come from heaven, to live on earth, and to die on the cross for your sins so that you can be with him forever.

DAY 3

May the God of hope fill you with all joy and peace in believing,
so that by the power of the Holy Spirit you may abound in hope.

ROMANS 15:13

As I write, we are entering the holiday season, which means the Christmas commercials started weeks ago. I actually kind of enjoy the commercials; they're always so festive and fun and ridiculously full of it.

Department store ads are the biggest culprits. They stick a bunch of smiley folks in fake snow and promise that gifting their khakis or cashmere to our loved ones is the perfect way to give joy this season. Sweaters equal joy, they say. And they're not even joking.

Thank goodness we know the truth.

Paul prayed that the God of hope would fill the Roman believers with "all joy and peace in believing" (Rom. 15:13).

In our commercial culture, this may sound like an empty, fluffy promise, but we know Paul wasn't an empty, fluffy guy. What he wrote, he believed. The certainty of joy and peace for followers of Jesus was Paul's experience and his great hope for the churches he ministered to.

Listen to his prayer for the Ephesians: "That you may know what is the hope to which he has called you, what are the riches of his glorious inheritance in the saints, and what is the immeasurable greatness of his power toward us who believe" (Eph. 1:18–19).

Note the powerful language: hope; a rich, glorious inheritance; immeasurable greatness. Add this to the joy and peace Paul promises in our passage this week, and we believers should be feeling pretty darn encouraged. God promises us wonderful things . . .

But there is a caveat.

It's only for those who believe.

"May the God of hope fill you with all joy and peace *in believing*" (Rom. 15:13, italics mine).

"His power toward us *who believe* . . ." (Eph. 1:19, italics mine).

It has been my personal experience that *distrust* destroys joy. When I doubt God's goodness or second-guess his methods or question what he's given me compared to someone else, I am dabbling in distrust and my joy and peace correspondingly tank. Never fails.

Sister, if we wonder why we lack hope or feel anxious, we must search our own hearts. Are we believing God? Are we trusting him?

Instead of khakis and cashmere, our God of hope promises joy and peace.

Our role is simply to take his word for it.

1. You've likely heard the expression "Comparison is the thief of joy." But what if it's really distrust that steals joy? What is the actual heart issue that we're dealing with when we compare ourselves to others?

_____

_____

_____

2. In what areas of your life are you struggling to believe God? Where are you trying to find joy apart from him? Pray over these things and ask him to strengthen you with joy.

_____

_____

_____

DAY 4

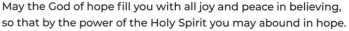

May the God of hope fill you with all joy and peace in believing,
so that by the power of the Holy Spirit you may abound in hope.

ROMANS 15:13

It's been a hard and heavy week.

I have wondered where in the world God is and why he tarries in answering my prayers. *Why can't you just make life easier, God? Why do we always have to wait?*

Isaiah 40:31 came to mind. I memorized it years ago in the NIV and often turn to it when I need a good kick in the pants to quit whining and start being strong in the Lord. "Those who hope in the LORD will renew their strength. They will soar on wings like eagles; they will run and not grow weary, they will walk and not be faint."

But this week I was suddenly struck by one tiny translation difference in the ESV that had *huge* implications. "But they who *wait* for the LORD shall renew their strength . . ." (italics mine).

It's fun to think of *hoping* in God and being strengthened. Hoping feels like the expectant promise of happy things to come. Right now things might be hard, but someday soon I'll soar, right?

But waiting? Well, *no one* likes waiting.

Yet, as I read on, I was surprised at how I had always misapplied this passage.

Waiting *is when we hope.*

It's *during the waiting* that our strength is renewed. Not after. Not once we've received what we were hoping for, but there in the middle of the hard. During the long, uncertain delay, *that's* when God strengthens us. *That's* when we soar on wings like eagles.

But how? Waiting is wearisome, physically and spiritually.

And God knows that.

Which is why our verse says it is "by the power of the Holy Spirit" alone that we can abound in hope (Rom. 15:13).

As we wait for whatever it is we're waiting for, we don't need to conjure up hope for ourselves. Hope is a gift of the Holy Spirit and yet another place we stand in awe and appreciation of what Jesus did on the cross.

Without his death, we have no hope for salvation. Without his resurrection, we have no hope for future glory. Without the Holy Spirit, we cannot abound in hope while on this earth, period.

Hope is a gift empowered by the Holy Spirit.

Praise God! Even in the waiting he gives good gifts.

1. Hoping and waiting are two sides of the same coin. Why do they feel different though? What can you do while you're waiting that will help you remember that this is where you soar?

_____

_____

_____

_____

2. Unbelievers don't have the power of the Holy Spirit to give them hope. How can remembering this help us relate to our non-Christian friends and family with compassion?

_____

_____

_____

DAY 5

May the God of hope fill you with all joy and peace in believing,
so that by the power of the Holy Spirit you may abound in hope.

ROMANS 15:13

Beloved sister, we have reached our final day together.

I wish I could sit down with you—over a white chocolate mocha, of course—and listen to your story. What has God taught you about himself in these weeks? Has he rearranged your heart like he has mine?

Each passage we've studied together was chosen by prayer and the Holy Spirit's prompting, and I have no doubt that he had *you* in mind as he led me to write. But you must know I often felt inadequate and unsure of the task ahead. Could twelve unrelated passages of Scripture fit together in one book? *Won't it feel disjointed, Lord? What will be the takeaway?*

But, as always, God is marvelously ahead of me.

As I look back now, I can see the way he wove a theme through our weeks that I did not expect and certainly didn't plan. He has even been so kind as to punctuate our time together finally and faithfully with the precious truths found in Romans 15:13, one last verse to speak to our hearts what I believe he longs for us to hear:

Through Christ alone, we are encouraged, expected, and even entitled to abound in hope.

This shouldn't surprise us. It's not some new, brilliant revelation. In fact, it's been God's Word to us all along.

"Whatever was written in former days was written for our instruction, that . . . through the encouragement of the Scriptures we might have hope" (Rom. 15:4).

The God of the universe, God Almighty, has written you the whole of his Word to tell you that he loves you. He knows you. He has good plans for you. *It's a promise.*

Your job is simply to believe.

Your reward is an abundance of hope.

Isn't this just the best news ever?

The truths of the Bible are for you, beloved. Please do not miss out on this gift.

Read his Word. Meditate on it. Hide it in your heart.

And—God promises—you *will* be blessed.

Let me close with one of my favorite verses, a verse God wrote for a specific woman long ago: Mary, the mother of Jesus. I believe these Holy Spirit–inspired words—spoken by Elizabeth, Mary's cousin—can still today be a treasured reminder for all of us that there is great joy found in trusting the Lord.

"Blessed is she who has believed that the Lord would fulfill his promises to her!" (Luke 1:45 NIV).

May we drink deeply of the promises in his Word, rejoice daily in an abundance of hope, and find our thirsty souls fully, wonderfully, beautifully satisfied in Jesus Christ alone.

1. Think on Luke 1:45. How does this encourage your heart to continue pressing on to know and trust in the Lord?

2. What will you do from here? Decide right now how you're going to continue to pursue the promises of the Lord found in his Word. You will be blessed!

DAY 6

May the God of hope fill you with all joy and peace in believing,
so that by the power of the Holy Spirit you may abound in hope.

ROMANS 15:13

Take a few minutes today to journal and reflect on what God revealed to your heart through our verse this week. What did you learn about yourself or God? Is there a sin you need to confess and turn from or a truth you need to apply to your life? How have you been changed by meditating on this passage?

DAY 7

May the God of hope fill you with all joy and peace in believing,
so that by the power of the Holy Spirit you may abound in hope.

ROMANS 15:13

*Close your week by praying the Word back to the Lord. Then rest! God's
promises are true. Let them satisfy and quiet your heart today.*

*Oh, Father, I praise you that you are the God of hope!
Fill me today with all joy and peace as I believe in you,
despite the hard and heavy times around me. Empower me
by your Holy Spirit to live every day of my life with a joy-
filled abundance of hope in Christ. Amen.*

ACKNOWLEDGMENTS

I had no idea how challenging it would be to be an author. It doesn't matter whether I'm trying to cram everything I want to say into a two-hundred-word board book or stretching every thought out to meet a thirty-thousand-word minimum; it's hard. Definitely not a one-woman job.

My incredible husband has shown me grace upon grace as I've learned and cried and doubted (and cried some more) and written and rewritten the words of this book. Josh Hall, you are a testimony to the truth of Ephesians 3:20. God gave immeasurably more than I could have ever asked for or imagined when he put you on my team. I love, love, love you.

My children, each one of you is evidence that the Lord gives the best gifts. What amazing little humans you are. I'm so grateful I get to be your mom. (Three hand squeezes . . .)

Dad and Mom, you set the bar high. Your legacy of loving God and loving others will live on long after the words have faded from these pages. And you're both just getting better and better. I'm so blessed to be a part of your story.

Julie Brents and Pat Hall, you love unconditionally, joyfully, and generously. And you taught your son to do the same. Thank you.

Sally Apokedak, God had an incredible surprise in store for me when he put us together. I sent you an email (with typos!) looking for an agent and ended up with a dear friend. Your faith encourages me, your wisdom sharpens me, and you have become like family. No, I did not see that coming, but I'm so very grateful it did.

Jennifer Patterson, why did it take us so long to find each other? You've prayed for me powerfully, stuck by me faithfully, pointed me to truth lovingly, and you still really seem to like me. God has been so kind to me through you. All those years I prayed for a sister, and you were right there all along.

Lindsey Brackett, Lynne Davis, Elizabeth Harper, Taryn Souders, and Janet Surette, writing is not necessarily a high-paying gig . . . until you consider the friendships. In that case, I am extraordinarily wealthy. I am oh so grateful for you all.

Laura Smith and Angela Story, gallons of coffee were consumed while you heard my heart and helped me carry this dream. Your accountability, friendship, and prayers were perfectly timed, life-giving, and life-changing. Thank you.

Mallory Hairston, Karen Hays, Jamie Marsh, Lindsey Owens, Lauren Shively, and Christy Steinmuller, it is an honor and pleasure to have done ministry with you over the years. Thank you for your faithfulness to the Lord and to his body.

Tara Abshier, Lydia Connor, Mackenzie Gies, Rachel Holland, Niki Junker-White, Sarah Phaneuf, Lindsey Taylor, and Andrea Wilson, you have each played such a precious role in loving, encouraging, and inspiring me. You ladies are so very dear to me.

Lori Ann Wood, your wise and gentle edits were such a blessing. You sacrificed your time—a commodity so precious I had no idea what a favor I was asking—to make this a better book. Your heart, my friend, is simply beautiful.

To my PGFirst family, thank you for allowing God to bless us through you. You have loved the Halls well.

Lynda Eubanks, Katie Lanier, Nicole Morehead, and Martha Strickland, thank you for loving and encouraging me across denominational lines. You are a beautiful example of the body of Christ in action.

David and Pam Parks, writing a book in the midst of a pandemic had its logistical challenges, but you generously came to the rescue. Thank you for providing me with a lovely cabin in which I could begin.

Tom and April Graney, you gave the generous getaway that was the perfect push I needed to finish. Thank you.

Rachel McRae and the Revell team, thank you for believing this newbie could stretch her child-size credentials into an adult-size dream. That's risky faith. I pray I'm worthy of it.

And to the fine folks at Briar Rose and Basecamp Coffee. Lots of words were written with your coffee in hand. And you weren't stingy with the cream either. Thank you.

NOTES

Week 1 Day 1

1. Jen Wilkin, *Women of the Word: How to Study the Bible with Both Our Hearts and Our Minds* (Wheaton: Crossway, 2014), 40.
2. "H1897. hagah," Strong's Hebrew Lexicon (KJV), Blue Letter Bible, accessed February 2, 2021, https://www.blueletterbible.org//lang/lexicon/lexicon.cfm?Strongs=H1897&t=KJV.

Week 1 Day 2

1. Chuck Smith, "Verse by Verse Study on Psalms 1–15 (C2000)," Blue Letter Bible, last modified June 1, 2005, https://www.blueletterbible.org/Comm/smith_chuck/c2000 _Psa/Psa_001.cfm.

Week 1 Day 4

1. C. H. Spurgeon, *The Treasury of David: Psalm 1*, Blue Letter Bible, accessed April 12, 2019, https://www.blueletterbible.org/Comm/spurgeon_charles/tod/ps001.cfm?a=479001.

Week 2 Day 1

1. Paul David Tripp, *Parenting: 14 Gospel Principles That Can Radically Change Your Family* (Wheaton: Crossway, 2016), 14.
2. John MacArthur, *The MacArthur Bible Commentary* (Nashville: Thomas Nelson, 2005), 1631.

Week 3 Day 2

1. "G5463. chairō," Strong's Greek Lexicon (KJV), Blue Letter Bible, accessed February 2, 2021, https://www.blueletterbible.org//lang/lexicon/lexicon.cfm?Strongs=G5463&t=KJV.

Week 3 Day 3

1. Philip Yancey, *Prayer: Does It Make Any Difference?* (Grand Rapids: Zondervan, 2006), 63.
2. Pastor John MacArthur, "Pray without Ceasing, Really?," audio sermon in The MacArthur Commentaries Series, Blue Letter Bible, accessed November 12, 2020, https://www .blueletterbible.org/audio_video/popPlayer.cfm?type=sa&id=91610154136&rel=Sermon Audio/MacArthur,%20John.

Week 4 Day 3

1. John Piper, "The Strength of a Godly Woman: Hope in Her God," Desiring God, September 22, 2017, https://www.desiringgod.org/messages/the-beautiful-faith-of-fearless-submission/excerpts/the-strength-of-a-godly-woman.

Week 5 Day 1

1. "I am the bread of life" (John 6:35, 41, 48, 51); "I am the light of the world" (8:12); "I am the door of the sheep" (10:7, 9); "I am the good shepherd" (10:11, 14); "I am the resurrection and the life" (11:25); "I am the way, and the truth, and the life" (14:6); "I am the true vine" (15:1, 5).

Week 5 Day 3

1. Brother Lawrence, *The Practice of the Presence of God* (New Kensington, PA: Whitaker House, 1982), 37, 48.

Week 5 Day 4

1. D. A. Carson, *The Pillar New Testament Commentary: The Gospel according to John* (Leicester: Apollos, 1991), accessed from Logos Bible Software.

Week 5 Day 5

1. Gerard L. Borchert, *The New American Commentary: John 12–21* (Nashville: B&H, 2002), accessed from Logos Bible Software.

Week 6 Day 1

1. A. W. Tozer, *The Knowledge of the Holy* (New York: HarperCollins, 1961), 1.

Week 8 Day 5

1. A. W. Pink, *The Sovereignty of God* (Blacksburg, VA: Wilder Productions, 2008), 11.

Week 11 Day 2

1. Joni Eareckson Tada, *Joni: An Unforgettable Story* (Grand Rapids: Zondervan, 1976).
2. Tada, *Joni*, 187.

ABOUT HANNAH

Hannah C. Hall is a wife to Josh, a mom to five, a caretaker of barnyard critters, and the world's okayest ukulele player. Ten years ago, Hannah's writing journey began with one little children's book that turned into eleven that turned into thirty-plus titles and over a million in sales. Whether Hannah is writing for kids or grown-ups, her heart is to proclaim God's goodness, and her hope is to spend her life inviting others to declare Psalm 34:3 alongside her: "Oh, magnify the LORD with me, and let us exalt his name together!" Find her online at hannahchall.com.

Get to know
Hannah

Head to *hannahchall.com* to learn more about Hannah,
find more of her books, or get in touch!

 Hannah C. Hall

 HannahCHall

 hannahchall1

Be the First to Hear about New Books from Revell!

Sign up for announcements about new and upcoming titles at

RevellBooks.com/SignUp

@RevellBooks

Don't miss out on our great reads!

Revell
a division of Baker Publishing Group
www.RevellBooks.com